KU-657-725

Cooking with Philly

A collection of delicious cooking and baking recipes to inspire and enjoy

pil
Publications International, Ltd.

Louis Weber, CEO
Publications International, Ltd.
7373 North Cicero Avenue
Lincolnwood, IL 60712

Special thanks to Kraft Foods:
Vice President Cheese & Dairy: Dan D'Alessandro
Brand Team: Farrah Bezner and Kelly Fleming
Culinary Lead: Cayla Runka

For nutritional information, go to www.kraftrecipes.com

Photography on pages 4, 7, 9, 11, 13, 15, 19, 31, 39, 41, 49, 55, 57, 59, 63, 69, 71, 73, 75, 104, 107, 109, 111, 148, 151, 157, 159, 195, 197, 199, and 201 by PIL Photo Studio, Chicago

Photographer: Annemarie Zelasko
Photographer's Assistants: Lauren Kessler, Sandy Rosencrans
Prop Stylist: Tom Hamilton
Food Stylists: Kim Hartman, Mary Ann Melone, Josephine Orba
Assistant Food Stylists: Sara Cruz, Brittany Culver, Breana Moeller

Pictured on the front cover: Red Velvet Cupcakes *(page 230)*.

Pictured on the inside front cover: Fettuccine Primavera *(page 72)*.

Pictured on the back cover (clockwise from top): Marinated Cheese Squares *(page 28)*, 20-Minute Skillet Salmon *(page 98)* and Brown Sugar Cheesecake with Bourbon Sauce *(page 196)*.

Pictured on the inside back cover: Bacon & Maple Scalloped Potatoes *(page 158)*.

ISBN: 978-1-4508-8576-8

Library of Congress Control Number: 2012932751

Manufactured in China.

8 7 6 5 4 3 2 1

Microwave Cooking: Microwave ovens vary in wattage. Use the cooking times as guidelines and check for doneness before adding more time.

Preparation/Cooking Times: Preparation times are based on the approximate amount of time required to assemble the recipe before cooking, baking, chilling, or serving. These times include preparation steps such as measuring, chopping, and mixing. The fact that some preparations and cooking can be done simultaneously is taken into account. Preparation of optional ingredients and serving suggestions is not included.

contents

Appetizers

Mini Salmon Cakes with Creamy Dill Sauce

prep: 20 min. \ total: 1 hour 12 min. \ makes: 24 servings, 2 cakes (40 g) and 1½ Tbsp. (22 ml) sauce each

- **1 tub (250 g) *Philadelphia* Dill Cream Cheese Product, divided**
- **1 egg**
- **3 green onions, sliced**
- **2 Tbsp. chopped Italian parsley**
- **1 Tbsp. lemon zest, divided**
- **1 Tbsp. lemon juice, divided**
- **2 cups/450 g flaked cooked salmon**
- **3 Tbsp. milk**
- **1 cup/ 125 g panko bread crumbs**
- **¼ cup/ 1/2 stick, 60 g butter, melted**

1 **Heat** oven to 400°F/ 200°C/mark 6.

2 **Mix** ½ cup/ 120 g cream cheese product and next 3 ingredients in medium bowl. Stir in 1 ½ tsp. each lemon zest and juice. Add salmon; mix lightly. (Mixture will be moist.) Refrigerate 30 min. Meanwhile, whisk remaining cream cheese, lemon zest, juice and milk until well blended. Refrigerate until ready to serve.

3 **Mix** panko crumbs and butter in shallow dish. Roll salmon mixture into 48 balls, using 1 Tbsp. for each. Roll in crumb mixture until evenly coated; place, 1 inch/ 2.5cm apart, on baking sheet sprayed with cooking spray. Flatten slightly with fork.

4 **Bake** 20 to 22 min. or until each salmon cake is golden brown on both sides, turning after 10 min. Serve with cream cheese sauce.

special extra

For more flavour, add 1 Tbsp. capers to the salmon mixture before rolling into balls.

Salmon Bites

prep: 10 min. \ total: 10 min. \ makes: 7 servings, 4 topped bread rounds (60 g) each

- **7 slices dense pumpernickel bread (250 g)**
- **½ cup (½ of 250-g tub) *Philadelphia* Dill Cream Cheese Product**
- **100 g smoked salmon**

1. **Use** 1¾-inch/5cm cookie cutter to cut 4 rounds out of each bread slice. Discard bread trimmings or reserve for another use.
2. **Spread** bread with cream cheese product; top with salmon.

special extra

Garnish each topped bread round with a sprig of fresh dill.

Roasted Sweet Potato & Garlic Soup

prep: 15 min. \ total: 1 hour 30 min. \ makes: 8 servings

- **2¼ lb. (1 kg) sweet potatoes (about 5), peeled, cut into 2-inch chunks**
- **2 onions, chopped**
- **1 head garlic, separated into cloves, peeled**
- **2 Tbsp. olive oil**
- **6 cups/ 1500 ml 25%-less-sodium chicken broth**
- **¼ cup/ 60 g *Philadelphia* Light Cream Cheese Spread**
- **2 Tbsp. chopped fresh chives**

1 **Heat** oven to 400°F/200°C/mark 6. Toss potatoes, onions and garlic with oil. Spread onto foil-covered baking sheet. Bake 1 hour or until vegetables are tender; spoon into large saucepan.

2 **Stir** in broth. Bring to boil on medium-high heat. Remove from heat; cool slightly. Add to blender, in batches, with cream cheese spread; blend until smooth. Return to saucepan.

3 **Cook** on medium heat until heated through, stirring occasionally. Serve topped with chives.

Zesty Stuffed Olives

prep: 10 min. \ total: 10 min. \ makes: 10 servings, 2 olives each

- **½ cup (½ of 250-g tub) *Philadelphia* Cream Cheese Spread**
- **20 colossal black olives**
- **2 Tbsp. Kraft Zesty Italian Dressing**
- **2 Tbsp. chopped fresh parsley**

1. **Spoon** cream cheese spread into small resealable plastic bag. Press cream cheese into one of the bottom corners of bag. Cut off small piece from corner of bag. Squeeze cream cheese into centres of olives.
2. **Place** olives on serving plate. Drizzle with dressing. Sprinkle with parsley.

Spring Veggie Pizza Appetizer

prep: 15 min. \ total: 2 hours 58 min. \ makes: 32 servings, 1/32 recipe (30 g) each

- **2 pkg. (235 g each) refrigerated crescent dinner rolls**
- **1 tub (250 g) *Philadelphia* Cream Cheese Spread**
- **½ cup / 125 g Miracle Whip Dressing**
- **1 tsp. dill weed**
- **½ tsp. onion salt**
- **1 cup/ 180 g each chopped sugar snap peas and quartered cherry tomatoes**
- **½ cup/90 g each sliced radishes, chopped yellow peppers and shredded carrots**
- **3 green onions, chopped**

1. **Heat** oven to 375°F/ 190°C/mark 5.
2. **Unroll** dough; separate into 4 rectangles. Press onto bottom and up sides of 15× 10× 1-inch/ 30x25x2 cm pan to form crust, firmly pressing seams and perforations together to seal.
3. **Bake** 11 to 13 min. or until golden brown; cool.
4. **Mix** cream cheese spread, dressing, dill weed and onion salt until well blended. Spread onto crust; top with remaining ingredients. Refrigerate 2 hours.

Festive Favourite Layered Dip

prep: 10 min. \ total: 10 min. \ makes: 6 cups dip or 48 servings, 2 Tbsp. (30 ml) dip and 7 crackers (25 g) each

- **1 tub (250 g) *Philadelphia* Cream Cheese Spread**
- **½ cup/125 g sour cream**
- **¼ cup/60 g Miracle Whip Dressing**
- **1 cup/270 g salsa**
- **2 cups/240 g Kraft Mozzarella Shredded Cheese**
- **1 green pepper, finely chopped**
- **2 tomatoes, chopped**
- **2 green onions, chopped**
- **Ritz Crackers**

1. **Mix** first 3 ingredients until well blended; spread into bowl.
2. **Top** with layers of all remaining ingredients except crackers.
3. **Serve** with crackers.

make ahead

Dip can be stored in refrigerator up to 2 hours before serving.

Mini Cheese Balls

prep: 10 min. \ total: 2 hours 10 min. \ makes: 18 servings, 3 cheese balls each

- **1 tub (250 g) *Philadelphia* Herb & Garlic Cream Cheese Spread**
- **1 pkg. (200 g) Kraft Mozzarella Shredded Cheese**
- **2 Tbsp. Oscar Mayer Real Bacon Bits**
- **½ tsp. Italian seasoning**
- **½ cup/60 g toasted walnuts, ground**

1. **Mix** cream cheese spread and mozzarella cheese until well blended. Stir in bacon bits and seasoning.
2. **Shape** mixture into 54 balls, 1 level tsp. each. Roll in walnuts. Cover with plastic wrap.
3. **Refrigerate** at least 2 hours.

make ahead

Make these ahead, wrap well and freeze up to 2 weeks ahead.

Baked Crab Rangoon

prep: 20 min. \ total: 40 min. \ makes: 12 servings, 1 rangoon (36 g) each

- **1 can (170 g) chunk crabmeat, drained, flaked**
- **125 g (½ of 250-g pkg.) *Philadelphia* Light Brick Cream Cheese Spread, softened**
- **¼ cup/60 g Miracle Whip Calorie-Wise Dressing**
- **2 green onions, thinly sliced**
- **12 won ton wrappers**

1. **Heat** oven to 350°F/ 180°C/mark 4.
2. **Mix** first 4 ingredients.
3. **Line** each of 12 muffin cups sprayed with cooking spray with 1 won ton wrapper, allowing edges of wrappers to extend over tops. Fill with crab mixture.
4. **Bake** 18 to 20 min. or until edges are golden brown and filling is heated through.

for crispier rangoons

Bake won ton wrappers in muffin cups at 350°F for 5 to 7 min. or until lightly browned. Fill with crabmeat mixture and bake 6 to 8 min. or until filling is heated through.

Chicken & Cranberry Bites

prep: 10 min. \ total: 25 min. \ makes: 24 servings, 1 square (33 g) each

- **1 pkg. (411 g) frozen puff pastry (2 blocks), thawed**
- **¾ cup (¾ of 250-g tub) *Philadelphia* Cream Cheese Spread**
- **1½ cups/225 g chopped cooked chicken breasts**
- **½ cup/ 135 g canned whole berry cranberry sauce**

1. **Heat** oven to 425°F/ 220°C/mark 7.
2. **Roll** out 1 pastry block on lightly floured surface into 12-inch square; cut into 12 squares. Place in single layer on lightly floured baking sheet. Repeat with remaining pastry block.
3. **Spoon** 1½ tsp. cream cheese spread onto centre of each pastry square. Top with chicken and cranberry sauce.
4. **Bake** 14 to 15 min. or until pasty is golden brown, rotating baking sheets after 7 min.

how to cut puff pastry:
Use a pizza cutter to easily cut the pastry dough into squares.

Fruit & Nut Bites

prep: 10 min. \ total: 10 min. \ makes: 6 servings

- **12 Ritz Crackers**
- **¼ cup/60 g *Philadelphia* Cream Cheese Spread**
- **2 Tbsp. Kraft Pure Apricot Jam**
- **2 Tbsp. toasted sliced almonds**

1. **Spread** crackers with cream cheese spread; top with jam.
2. **Sprinkle** with almonds.

substitute

Substitute hot pepper jelly for the apricot jam.

Pesto Crostini

prep: 15 min. \ total: 15 min. \ makes: 18 servings, 2 crostini (31 g) each

- **3 cups/120 g loosely packed fresh basil**
- **⅓ cup/80 ml Kraft Signature Classic Herb Dressing**
- **⅓ cup/35 g Kraft 100% Parmesan Grated Cheese**
- **1 baguette (20 inch), ends trimmed, cut into 36 slices and toasted**
- **2 pkg. (250 g each) *Philadelphia* Cream Cheese Spread**

1. **Process** basil, dressing and Parmesan in food processor until well blended.
2. **Spread** cream cheese spread onto toast slices.
3. **Top** with basil mixture.

special extra

Top with additional Parmesan before serving.

Marinated Cheese Squares

prep: 10 min. \ total: 1 hour 10 min. \ makes: 16 servings, 2 cream cheese pieces (25 g) each

- **1 pkg. (250 g) *Philadelphia* Brick Cream Cheese**
- **½ cup/120 ml Kraft Extra Virgin Olive Oil Fig Balsamic Dressing**
- **2 Tbsp. chopped fresh parsley**
- **1 Tbsp. finely chopped red onions**
- **1 tsp. lime zest**
- **½ tsp. cracked black pepper**

1. **Cut** cream cheese into 32 pieces; place in shallow dish.
2. **Mix** remaining ingredients.
3. **Pour** dressing mixture over cream cheese. Refrigerate 1 hour.

serving suggestion

Serve with assorted Christie Crackers or baguette slices.

Creamy Mediterranean Spread

prep: 10 min. \ total: 10 min. \ makes: 3 cups spread or 24 servings, 2 Tbsp. spread (30 ml) and 6 crackers (20 g) each

1 pkg. (250 g) *Philadelphia* Brick Cream Cheese, softened

1 jar (360 g) roasted red peppers, drained, chopped

1 pkg. (200 g) Kraft Feta with Oregano, Sun Dried Tomatoes and Cracked Peppercorns Cheese

½ cup/90 g chopped kalamata olives

¼ cup/ 60 ml Kraft Extra Virgin Olive Oil Aged Balsamic Vinaigrette Dressing

2 Tbsp. chopped fresh parsley

Ritz Crackers

1 **Spread** cream cheese onto bottom of pie plate.

2 **Combine** all remaining ingredients except crackers; spoon over cream cheese.

3 **Serve** with crackers.

Salsa Roll-Ups

prep: 15 min. \ total: 15 min. \ makes: 9 servings, 2 slices (36 g) each

125 g (½ of 250-g pkg.) *Philadelphia* Light Brick Cream Cheese Spread, softened

3 Tbsp. salsa

2 large spinach-flavoured tortillas

½ cup/60 g shredded Cracker Barrel Cheddar Cheese Light

½ tsp. chili powder

1. **Mix** cream cheese spread and salsa; spread onto tortillas.
2. **Top** with shredded cheese and chili powder; roll up tightly.
3. **Cut** each roll-up into 9 slices.

make ahead

Prepare roll-ups as directed, but do not cut into slices. Tightly wrap each roll-up in plastic wrap. Refrigerate up to 4 hours. Slice just before serving.

Sweet 'N Hot Cheese Spread

prep: 5 min. \ total: 6 min. \ makes: 1¼ cups spread or 10 servings, 2 Tbsp. (30 ml) spread and 6 crackers (20 g) each

- **1 pkg. (250 g) *Philadelphia* Brick Cream Cheese, softened**
- **3 Tbsp. Kraft Pure Apricot Jam**
- **⅛ tsp. cayenne pepper**
- **¼ cup/30 g slivered almonds**
- **Ritz Crackers**

1. **Spread** cream cheese onto bottom of microwaveable quiche dish or pie plate.
2. **Top** with jam; sprinkle with pepper and nuts.
3. **Microwave** on HIGH 1 min. or until heated through. Serve with crackers.

substitute

Substitute Kraft Pure Orange Marmalade for the apricot jam.

Rustic Carmelized Onion Tart

prep: 10 min. \ total: 1 hour \ makes: 10 servings, 1 piece (79 g) each

- **4 slices bacon, cut into 1-inch pieces**
- **1 large onion, thinly sliced**
- **1 ready-to-use refrigerated pie crust (½ of 400-g pkg.)**
- **1 pkg. (250 g) *Philadelphia* Brick Cream Cheese, softened**
- **¼ cup/60 g sour cream**
- **½ cup/60 g shredded Swiss cheese**

1. **Cook** bacon in large skillet on medium-high heat 5 min. or just until bacon is crisp, stirring occasionally. Remove bacon from skillet with slotted spoon, reserving drippings in skillet. Drain bacon on paper towels; set aside. Add onions to drippings; cook 15 to 20 min. or until onions are caramelized, stirring frequently.
2. **Heat** oven to 400°F/ 200°C/mark 6. Unroll pie crust on baking sheet. Mix cream cheese and sour cream; spread onto crust. Spoon onion mixture and bacon onto centre of crust, leaving 2-inch/5cm border; top with Swiss cheese. Fold border over filling, leaving opening in centre and pleating crust as necessary to fit.
3. **Bake** 20 to 25 min. or until crust is lightly browned. Cool slightly.

special extra:

For a touch of sweetness, add 1 Tbsp. orange marmalade to cooked onion mixture before spooning over cream cheese mixture on pie crust.

Artichoke-Cheese Puffs

prep: 10 min. \ total: 55 min. \ makes: 16 servings, 2 puffs each

- **42 Ritz Crackers, divided**
- **1 pkg. (250 g) *Philadelphia* Brick Cream Cheese, softened**
- **¼ cup/25 g Kraft 100% Parmesan Grated Cheese**
- **¼ cup/30 g Kraft Mozzarella Shredded Cheese**
- **½ cup/90 g chopped drained canned artichoke hearts**

1. **Crush** 10 crackers; place crumbs in shallow dish. Mix cheeses and artichokes; shape into 32 balls, using 2 tsp. for each ball. Coat with crumbs; place in shallow pan. Refrigerate 30 min.
2. **Heat** oven to 350°F / 180°C/mark 4. Place remaining crackers in single layer on baking sheet; top each with 1 cheese ball.
3. **Bake** 15 min. or until heated through.

special extra

Add finely chopped red, green and yellow peppers to the crumbs before using to coat cheese balls as directed.

Layered Sun-Dried Tomato and Artichoke Spread

prep: 10 min. \ total: 1 hour 10 min. \ makes: 1½ cups spread or 12 servings, 2 Tbsp (30 ml) spread and 6 crackers (20 g) each

1 pkg. (250 g) *Philadelphia* Brick Cream Cheese, well chilled

3 Tbsp. finely chopped sun-dried tomatoes in oil, well drained

3 Tbsp. finely chopped drained canned artichoke hearts

2 Tbsp. pesto

2 Tbsp. chopped Back to Nature Sea Salt Roasted Almonds

2 tsp. chopped fresh parsley

Ritz Crackers

1. **Cut** cream cheese horizontally into 3 slices using dental floss. (See Tip.) Place 1 slice on large sheet of plastic wrap; top with tomatoes and second cream cheese slice.
2. **Combine** artichokes and pesto; spoon over second cream cheese layer.
3. **Top** with remaining cream cheese slice, nuts and parsley; press nuts and parsley lightly into cream cheese to secure. Wrap with plastic wrap. Refrigerate 1 hour. Serve with crackers.

how to cut cream cheese with dental floss

Wrap 18-inch piece of dental floss around bottom third of cream cheese brick, overlapping ends. Pull ends steadily to cut cream cheese. Repeat to make a total of 3 slices.

Savoury Three-Cheese Spread

prep: 9 min. \ total: 10 min. \ makes: 10 servings

- **1 pkg. (250 g) *Philadelphia* Brick Cream Cheese, softened**
- **1 cup/120 g Kraft Double Cheddar Shredded Cheese**
- **3 slices (30 g) deli smoked ham, finely chopped**
- **¼ cup/25 g Kraft 100% Parmesan Grated Cheese**
- **1 Tbsp. chopped red peppers**
- **1 Tbsp. sliced green onions**
- **¼ tsp. cayenne pepper**

1. **Spread** cream cheese onto bottom of 2½-cup/600 ml microwaveable dish. Sprinkle with Cheddar cheese, ham and Parmesan cheese.
2. **Microwave** on HIGH 1 min. or until heated through.
3. **Top** spread with red peppers, onions and cayenne pepper. Serve with Ritz Crackers.

substitute

Switch sliced jalapeño peppers, chopped roasted red peppers or salsa for any of the toppings for a different flavour combo.

Cheese Truffles

prep: 15 min. \ total: 3 hours 15 min. \ makes: 4 doz. or 24 servings, 2 truffles (36 g) and 5 crackers (13 g) each

- **2 pkg. (250 g each) *Philadelphia* Brick Cream Cheese, softened**
- **1 pkg. (200 g) Kraft Double Cheddar Shredded Cheese**
- **1 tsp. garlic powder**
- **Dash cayenne pepper**
- **¼ cup/45 g chopped roasted red peppers**
- **2 green onions, chopped**
- **1⅔ cups/200 g chopped pecans**
- **Christie Sociables Original Crackers**

1. **Beat** first 4 ingredients with mixer until blended. Divide in half. Add roasted peppers to half and onions to other half; mix each until blended.
2. **Refrigerate** several hours or until chilled.
3. **Shape** into 48 (1-inch/2.5 cm) balls. Roll in nuts. Refrigerate until ready to serve. Serve with crackers.

cheese logs

Roll each half into 6-inch log before coating with nuts.

Cream Cheese-Bacon Crescents

prep: 15 min. \ total: 30 min. \ makes: 16 servings, 2 crescents (45 g) each

- **1 tub (250 g) *Philadelphia* Herb & Garlic Cream Cheese Spread**
- **2 Tbsp. Oscar Mayer Real Bacon Bits**
- **2 cans (235 g each) refrigerated crescent dinner rolls**

1. **Heat** oven to 375°F/ 190°C/mark 5.
2. **Mix** cream cheese spread and bacon bits until well blended.
3. **Separate** each can of dough into 8 triangles. Cut each triangle lengthwise in half. Spread each dough triangle with 1 generous tsp. cream cheese mixture. Roll up, starting at short side of triangle. Place, point-sides down, on baking sheet.
4. **Bake** 12 to 15 min. or until golden brown. Serve warm.

variation

For a sweet version, prepare using *Philadelphia* Strawberry Light Cream Cheese Spread and substituting chopped walnuts for the bacon bits.

Easy-Bake Cheddar Biscuits

prep: 10 min. \ total: 22 min. \ makes: 9 servings, 1 biscuit and 1 Tbsp. cream cheese product each

- **1 cup flour**
- **2 tsp. Magic Baking Powder**
- **¼ tsp. cream of tartar**
- **¼ tsp. sugar**
- **¼ tsp. salt**
- **¼ cup/30 g cold butter, cubed**
- **1 cup/120 g Kraft Double Cheddar Shredded Cheese**
- **⅓ cup/110 ml plus 2 Tbsp. milk**
- **9 Tbsp. *Philadelphia* Chive & Onion Cream Cheese Product, divided**

1. **Heat** oven to 450°F/230°C/mark 8. Mix flour, baking powder, cream of tartar, sugar and salt in medium bowl. Cut in butter with pastry blender or 2 knives until mixture resembles coarse crumbs. Stir in Cheddar. Add milk; stir until mixture forms soft dough.
2. **Place** on lightly floured surface; knead 8 to 10 times or until smooth. Pat dough into 6-inch/15 cm square; cut into 9 smaller squares. Place, 2 inches/5 cm apart, on baking sheet.
3. **Bake** 10 to 12 min. or until golden brown. Cut in half; spread with cream cheese product.

Caramelized Onion & Olive Tart

prep: 40 min. \ total: 55 min. \ makes: 16 servings

- **2 large sweet onions, thinly sliced**
- **3 Tbsp. Kraft Signature Balsamic Vinaigrette Dressing**
- **1 sheet frozen puff pastry (½ of 397-g pkg.), thawed**
- **½ cup (½ of 250-g tub) *Philadelphia* Cream Cheese Spread**
- **½ cup/90 g pitted kalamata olives, cut in half**
- **¼ cup/25 g Kraft 100% Parmesan Grated Cheese**
- **1 Tbsp. chopped fresh thyme**

1. **Heat** oven to 400°F/ 230°C/mark 8. Cook onions in dressing in large covered skillet on medium-low heat 25 min. or until tender, stirring occasionally. Remove from heat; set aside to cool.
2. **Meanwhile,** roll pastry into 12-inch/30 cm square on lightly floured surface. Place in parchment-lined 15×10×¾-inch/30×25×2 cm pan. Spread with cream cheese spread to within 1 inch of edges; top with remaining ingredients.
3. **Bake** 15 min. or until pastry is golden brown. Serve warm or cooled to room temperature.

substitute

Prepare with phyllo dough instead. Layer 4 sheets of phyllo, brushing lightly with melted butter between the layers. Continue as directed, baking 18 to 20 min. or until golden brown.

Cool & Creamy Crab Dip

prep: 15 min. \ total: 15 min. \ makes: 2 cups dip or 16 servings, 2 Tbsp. (30 ml) dip, 3 pea pods (10 g) and 2 crackers (4 g) each

- **1 tub (250 g) *Philadelphia* Spinach Light Cream Cheese Product**
- **⅓ cup/80 g Miracle Whip Calorie-Wise Dressing**
- **1 cup/225 g chopped cooked crabmeat**
- **2 tsp. lemon juice**
- **2 green onions, chopped**
- **1½ cups/250 g fresh sugar snap peas**
- **Triscuit Thin Crisps Original Crackers**

1. **Mix** cream cheese product and dressing in medium bowl until well blended.
2. **Stir** in next 3 ingredients.
3. **Serve** with peas and crackers.

Smoked Salmon Dip

prep: 10 min. \ total: 10 min. \ makes: 16 servings

- **1 tub (250 g) *Philadelphia* Cream Cheese Spread**
- **⅓ cup/80 g Kraft Mayo Real Mayonnaise**
- **⅓ cup/80 g sour cream**
- **90 g smoked salmon, chopped (about ½ cup)**
- **Grated zest from 1 lemon (about 1 Tbsp.)**

1. **Mix** cream cheese spread, mayonnaise and sour cream until well blended.
2. **Add** salmon and lemon zest; stir gently until well blended.
3. **Serve** with Christie Wheat Thin Crackers.

jazz it up

Add 2 Tbsp. finely chopped fresh dill along with the salmon and lemon zest.

Cucumber Roulades

prep: 10 min. \ total: 10 min. \ makes: 6 servings, 2 topped cucumber slices (32 g) each

- **1 English cucumber, peeled**
- **¼ cup/60 g *Philadelphia* Chive & Onion Cream Cheese Product**
- **30 g smoked salmon, thinly sliced, cut into 12 pieces**
- **12 sprigs fresh dill**

1. **Cut** cucumber into 12 thick slices. Use melon baller to scoop out centre of each.
2. **Fill** with cream cheese product; top with salmon and dill.

substitute

Substitute 12 drained canned baby shrimp for the salmon.

Reuben Spread

prep: 15 min. \ total: 35 min. \ makes: 2½ cups spread or 20 servings, 2 Tbsp. (30 ml) spread and 4 crackers (18 g) each

125 g (½ of 250-g pkg.) *Philadelphia* Brick Cream Cheese, softened

½ cup/120 g Kraft Thousand Island Dressing

¼ lb. (125 g) sliced deli corned beef, chopped (about 1 cup)

¾ cup/200 g well-drained sauerkraut

3 cups/360 g shredded Kraft Swiss Cheese

Triscuit Rye with Caraway Seeds Crackers

1 **Heat** oven to 350°F/ 180°C/mark 4.

2 **Mix** cream cheese and dressing in medium bowl; stir in all remaining ingredients except crackers.

3 **Spread** onto bottom of 9-inch/23 cm pie plate or shallow dish.

4 **Bake** 20 min. or until heated through. Serve warm with crackers.

shortcut

Instead of baking prepared spread, microwave in microwaveable shallow dish on HIGH 2 to 3 min. or until heated through.

Party Cheese Ball

prep: 15 min. \ total: 3 hours 15 min. \ makes: 3 cups or 24 servings, 2 Tbsp. (30 ml) each

- **2 pkg. (250 g each) *Philadelphia* Brick Cream Cheese, softened**
- **2 cups/240 g Kraft Old Cheddar Shredded Cheese**
- **1 Tbsp. finely chopped onions**
- **1 Tbsp. chopped red peppers**
- **2 tsp. Worcestershire sauce**
- **1 tsp. lemon juice**
- **Dash cayenne pepper**
- **1 cup/120 g chopped pecans, toasted**

1. **Beat** cream cheese and Cheddar in small bowl with mixer until well blended.
2. **Add** all remaining ingredients except nuts; mix well. Refrigerate several hours.
3. **Shape** into ball; roll in nuts.

serving suggestion

Serve with Ritz Crackers and/or Christie Wheat Thin Crackers.

Hot Oniony Cheese Dip

prep: 25 min. \ total: 45 min. \ makes: 2¼ cups or 18 servings, 2 Tbsp. (30 ml) dip each

- **1 pkg. (250 g) PHILADELPHIA Brick Cream Cheese, softened**
- **⅓ cup/80 g Miracle Whip Dressing**
- **1 Tbsp. dry onion soup mix**
- **1 cup/120 g Kraft Part Skim Mozzarella Shredded Cheese**
- **⅓ cup/30 g sliced almonds, toasted**

1. **Heat** oven to 350°F/180°C/mark 4.
2. **Mix** first 3 ingredients in medium bowl. Stir in mozzarella.
3. **Spoon** into ovenproof serving dish.
4. **Bake** 15 to 20 min. or until heated through, stirring after 8 min. Top with nuts.

serving suggestions

Serve with fresh vegetable dippers, Triscuit Thin Crisps Crackers and/or Christie Wheat Thin Crackers.

Savoury Parmesan Bites

prep: 15 min. \ total: 30 min. \ makes: 32 servings, 1 bite (25 g) each

- **1 pkg. (250 g) *Philadelphia* Brick Cream Cheese, softened**
- **1 cup/110 g Kraft 100% Parmesan Grated Cheese, divided**
- **2 cans (235 g each) refrigerated crescent dinner rolls**
- **1 cup/180 g chopped red peppers**
- **¼ cup/10 g chopped fresh parsley**

1. **Heat** oven to 350°F/180°C/mark 4.
2. **Beat** cream cheese and ¾ cup/85 g Parmesan with mixer until well blended.
3. **Separate** rolls into 4 rectangles; press perforations together to seal. Spread 3 Tbsp. cream cheese mixture onto each rectangle; top with peppers and parsley. Fold 1 long side of each rectangle over filling to centre; fold up again to enclose remaining filling. Cut each into 8 squares. Place, seam-sides down, on baking sheet. Sprinkle with remaining Parmesan.
4. **Bake** 13 to 15 min. or until golden brown.

Simple Meals

Vegetable Chowder

prep: 15 min. \ total: 45 min. \ makes: 8 servings, 1 cup (250 ml) each

- **2 Tbsp./30 g oil**
- **1 small onion, chopped**
- **2 cloves garlic, minced**
- **1 carrot, peeled, chopped**
- **1 cup/180 g coarsely chopped cauliflower florets**
- **1 large potato (225 g), peeled, chopped**
- **2 cups/500 ml 25%-less-sodium chicken broth**
- **2 cups/500 ml milk**
- **½ cup/90 g frozen corn**
- **1 tub (250 g) *Philadelphia* Dill Cream Cheese Product**

1. **Heat** oil in large saucepan on medium-high heat. Add onions and garlic; cook and stir 2 to 3 min. or until crisp-tender. Add carrots, cauliflower and potatoes; cook and stir 3 min.
2. **Stir** in broth, milk and corn. Bring to boil; cover. Simmer on medium-low heat 8 to 10 min. or until vegetables are tender.
3. **Add** cream cheese product; cook and stir 5 min. or until melted. (Do not let soup come to boil.)

special extra

Garnish each serving with 1 tsp. each chopped green onions or fresh chives.

Ham & Cheese Breakfast Mini Quiches

prep: 15 min. \ total: 45 min. \ makes: 6 servings, 2 quiches each

- **12 slices whole wheat bread**
- **4 eggs**
- **½ cup (½ of 250-g tub) *Philadelphia* Light Cream Cheese Spread**
- **1 Tbsp. milk**
- **60 g deli smoked ham, chopped**
- **2 green onions, sliced**

1. **Heat** oven to 400°F/ 200°C/mark 6. Use rolling pin to flatten each bread slice to 5-inch/ 12.5 cm square. Cut out centres with 3½-inch/9 cm round cookie cutter. Discard trimmings or reserve for another use. Press 1 bread circle onto bottom and up side of each of 12 greased muffin cups. Bake 8 to 10 min. or until golden brown.
2. **Reduce** oven temperature to 350°F / 180°C/mark 4. Meanwhile, beat 1 of the eggs and the cream cheese spread in medium bowl with wire whisk until well blended. Add remaining 3 eggs, the milk, ham and onions; mix well. Pour cream cheese mixture evenly into bread cups.
3. **Bake** 18 to 20 min. or until filling in centre of each cup is set. Serve warm.

Fettuccine Primavera

prep: 15 min. \ total: 30 min. \ makes: 4 servings, 1½ cups (375 ml) each

- **220 g fettuccine, uncooked**
- **1 Tbsp. oil**
- **1 lb. (450 g) fresh asparagus spears, trimmed, cut into 2-inch lengths**
- **1 small zucchini, sliced**
- **2 cloves garlic, minced**
- **½ cup (½ of 250-g tub) *Philadelphia* Dill Cream Cheese Product**
- **¾ cup/185 ml 25%-less-sodium chicken broth**
- **3 green onions, sliced**
- **1 Tbsp. lemon juice**
- **¼ tsp. black pepper**

1. **Cook** pasta as directed on package, omitting salt. Meanwhile, heat oil in large nonstick skillet on medium-high heat. Add asparagus, zucchini and garlic; cook and stir 2 to 3 min. or until crisp-tender. Spoon vegetables to one side of skillet.
2. **Add** cream cheese product and broth to other side of skillet; cook and stir 3 to 4 min. or until cream cheese is melted. Add onions and lemon juice; stir to evenly coat all ingredients in skillet with sauce. Cook and stir 1 to 2 min. or until heated through.
3. **Drain** pasta; place in large bowl. Add vegetable mixture; mix lightly. Sprinkle with pepper.

adding protein

Add cooked shrimp, smoked salmon or leftover cooked salmon to this vegetarian pasta for added protein.

Mediterranean Frittata

prep: 10 min. \ total: 50 min. \ makes: 6 servings, 1 wedge (119 g) each

- **5 eggs, beaten**
- **½ cup (½ of 250-g tub) *Philadelphia* 95% Fat Free Cream Cheese Product**
- **2 Tbsp. pesto**
- **2 cloves garlic, minced**
- **½ cup/60 g Kraft Part Skim Mozzarella Shredded Cheese**
- **1 zucchini, shredded**
- **1 tomato, chopped**
- **3 green onions, sliced**

1. **Heat** oven to 350°F/ 180°C/mark 4.
2. **Mix** all ingredients until well blended.
3. **Spoon** into greased 9-inch/23 cm pie plate.
4. **Bake** 40 min. or until centre is set. Let stand 5 min. before cutting into 6 wedges to serve.

variation

For a change of pace, substitute shredded Kraft Swiss Cheese for the Kraft Part Skim Mozzarella Shredded Cheese and 1 cup/180 g drained, canned stewed tomatoes for the chopped fresh tomato.

Spaghetti

prep: 25 min. \ total: 25 min. \ makes: 4 servings, 1½ cups (375 ml) each

- **225 g spaghetti, uncooked**
- **1 lb. (450 g) extra-lean ground beef**
- **2½ cups/650 g spaghetti sauce**
- **125 g (½ of 250-g pkg.) *Philadelphia* Light Brick Cream Cheese Spread, cubed**
- **2 Tbsp. Kraft 100% Parmesan Grated Cheese**

1. **Cook** spaghetti as directed on package, omitting salt.
2. **Meanwhile,** brown meat in large skillet. Stir in sauce and cream cheese spread; cook on low heat 3 to 5 min. or until sauce is well blended and heated through, stirring frequently.
3. **Drain** spaghetti. Add to sauce; mix lightly. Place on platter; top with Parmesan.

special extra

Sprinkle with chopped fresh basil or parsley before serving.

Chicken-Parmesan Bundles

prep: 35 min. \ total: 1 hour 5 min. \ makes: 6 servings, ⅙ recipe (236 g) each

- **125 g (½ of 250-g pkg.) *Philadelphia* Brick Cream Cheese, softened**
- **1 pkg. (300 g) frozen chopped spinach, thawed, well drained**
- **1¼ cups/150 g Kraft Mozzarella Shredded Cheese, divided**
- **6 Tbsp. Kraft 100% Parmesan Grated Cheese, divided**
- **6 small boneless skinless chicken breasts (1½ lb./675 g), pounded to ¼-inch/6 mm thickness**
- **1 egg**
- **10 Ritz Crackers, crushed (about ⅓ cup)**
- **1½ cups/400 g pasta sauce**

1. **Heat** oven to 375°F/190°C/mark 5.
2. **Mix** cream cheese, spinach, 1 cup/120 g mozzarella and 3 Tbsp. Parmesan until well blended; spread onto chicken breasts. Starting at 1 short end of each breast, roll up chicken tightly. Secure with wooden toothpicks, if desired.
3. **Beat** egg in pie plate. Mix remaining Parmesan and cracker crumbs in separate pie plate. Dip chicken, 1 at a time, in egg, then roll in crumb mixture. Place, seam-sides down, in 13×9-inch/33×23 cm baking dish sprayed with cooking spray.
4. **Bake** 30 min. or until chicken is done (170°F/77°C), heating pasta sauce near the end of the chicken baking time. Discard toothpicks. Serve chicken topped with pasta sauce and remaining mozzarella.

special extra

Sprinkle with chopped fresh basil before serving.

Potato-Topped Mini Meatloaves

prep: 15 min. \ total: 40 min. \ makes: 4 servings, 2 topped meatloaves (360 g) each

- **1 lb. (450 g) extra-lean ground beef**
- **1 pkg. (120 g) Stove Top Lower Sodium Stuffing Mix for Chicken**
- **1 cup/250 ml water**
- **125 g (½ of 250-g pkg.) *Philadelphia* Brick Cream Cheese, cubed**
- **2 cloves garlic, minced**
- **2 cups/420 g hot mashed potatoes**
- **¼ cup/10 g chopped fresh parsley**
- **1 can (284 ml/10 fl. oz.) beef gravy, warmed**

1. **Heat** oven to 375°F/190°C/mark 5.
2. **Mix** meat, stuffing mix and water; press into 8 muffin cups sprayed with cooking spray.
3. **Bake** 20 to 25 min. or until done (160°F/70°C).
4. **Add** cream cheese and garlic to potatoes; stir until cream cheese is melted. Stir in parsley. Scoop over meatloaves. Serve with gravy.

Criss-Cross Shepherd's Pie

prep: 30 min. \ total: 58 min. \ makes: 8 servings, 1¼ cups (300 ml) each

- **1½ lb. (675 g) Yukon Gold potatoes (about 3 large), peeled, cut into 1-inch chunks**
- **2 cloves garlic**
- **2 lb. (900 g) extra-lean ground beef**
- **2 onions, chopped**
- **2 cups/360 g frozen corn, thawed, drained**
- **1 cup/250 ml water**
- **1 pkg. (55 g) onion soup mix**
- **1 cup/120 g Kraft Old Cheddar Shredded Cheese**
- **¼ cup/60 g *Philadelphia* Cream Cheese Spread**

1. **Heat** oven to 375°F/ 190°C/mark 5.
2. **Cook** potatoes and garlic in boiling water in large saucepan 15 min. or until potatoes are tender. Meanwhile, brown meat with onions in large skillet; drain. Return to skillet. Stir in corn, water and soup mix; cook 3 min. or until water is absorbed, stirring frequently. Spoon into 8 ramekins.
3. **Drain** potatoes; return to saucepan. Add Cheddar and cream cheese spread; mash until potatoes are smooth and mixture is well blended. Spoon over meat mixture. Make decorative criss-cross or cross-hatch pattern by lightly dragging fork over potato layer.
4. **Bake** 15 to 20 min. or until heated through.

make ahead

Assemble recipe as directed; cover with heavy-duty foil. Freeze up to 1 month. When ready to serve, thaw overnight in refrigerator. Bake, covered, 25 to 30 min. or until heated through, uncovering the last 10 min.

Creamy Mustard Chicken

prep: 5 min. \ total: 30 min. \ makes: 4 servings, 1 chicken breast (115 g) each

- **1 tsp. oil**
- **4 small boneless skinless chicken breasts (1 lb./450 g)**
- **⅓ cup/85 ml 25%-less-sodium chicken broth**
- **¼ cup/60 g *Philadelphia* Cream Cheese Spread**
- **1 Tbsp. old-style mustard**

1. **Heat** oil in large nonstick skillet on medium heat. Add chicken; cook 6 to 8 min. on each side or until done (170°F/77°C). Transfer to plate; cover to keep warm.
2. **Add** broth to skillet; cook on medium heat 3 to 5 min. or until hot. Add cream cheese spread and mustard; cook and stir 2 to 3 min. or until cream cheese is completely melted and sauce is well blended and slightly thickened.
3. **Pour** sauce over chicken.

serving suggestion

Serve with potatoes, hot cooked rice or pasta and your favourite cooked vegetable.

Creamy Basil & Red Pepper Pasta

prep: 10 min. \ total: 25 min. \ makes: 4 servings

- **2 cups/240 g whole wheat penne pasta, uncooked**
- **1 jar (300 g) roasted red peppers, well drained**
- **½ cup (½ of 250-g tub) *Philadelphia* Light Cream Cheese Spread**
- **½ cup/125 ml skim milk**
- **½ cup/20 g fresh basil**
- **2 Tbsp. Kraft 100% Parmesan Light Grated Cheese**
- **1 lb. (450 g) boneless skinless chicken breasts, cut into bite-size pieces**

1. **Cook** pasta as directed on package. Meanwhile, blend all remaining ingredients except chicken in blender until smooth.
2. **Spray** large skillet with cooking spray. Add chicken; cook on medium-high heat 3 min., stirring frequently. Stir in pepper mixture; simmer on medium heat 5 min. or until heated through, stirring frequently.
3. **Drain** pasta. Add to chicken mixture; mix lightly.

special extra

Top with additional fresh basil leaves.

Croque Monsieur

prep: 5 min. \ total: 5 min. \ makes: 2 servings

- **2 thick slices crusty bread**
- **2 Tbsp. *Philadelphia* Herb & Garlic Cream Cheese Spread**
- **80 g sliced deli Black Forest ham**
- **2 Cracker Barrel Swiss Cheese Slices**

1. **Heat** broiler.
2. **Place** bread on baking sheet. Broil, 3 inches from heat source, 30 sec. or until toasted. Turn.
3. **Spread** with cream cheese spread; top with ham and cheese.
4. **Broil** 30 sec. or until cheese is melted.

serving suggestion

Serve with a crisp green salad tossed with your favourite Kraft Dressing.

Fiesta Chicken Enchiladas Made Over

prep: 15 min. \ total: 48 min. \ makes: 4 servings, 2 enchiladas (280 g) each

- **1 lb. (450 g) boneless skinless chicken breasts, cut into bite-size pieces**
- **1 each large green and red pepper, chopped**
- **1 Tbsp. chili powder**
- **¾ cup/200 g salsa, divided**
- **63 g (about ¼ of 250 g-pkg.) *Philadelphia* Light Brick Cream Cheese Spread, cubed**
- **¾ cup/90 g Kraft Tex Mex Light Shredded Cheese, divided**
- **8 small whole wheat tortillas**

1. **Heat** oven to 375°F/ 190°C/mark 5.
2. **Heat** large skillet sprayed with cooking spray on medium heat. Add chicken, peppers and chili powder; cook and stir 8 min. or until chicken is done (170°F/77°C). Stir in ¼ cup/70 g salsa and cream cheese spread; cook and stir 3 to 5 min. or until cream cheese is melted and mixture is well blended. Stir in ¼ cup/30 g shredded cheese.
3. **Spoon** heaping ⅓ cup/85 ml chicken mixture down centre of each tortilla; roll up. Place, seam-sides down, in 13×9-inch/33×23 cm baking dish sprayed with cooking spray; top with remaining salsa and shredded cheese. Cover.
4. **Bake** 20 min. or until heated through.

variation

Prepare using corn tortillas. To prevent cracking, warm tortillas as directed on package before filling and baking as directed.

Roast Pork Tenderloin Supper

prep: 20 min.\ total: 45 min.\ makes 4 servings, ¼ recipe (272 g) each

- **1 pork tenderloin (1 lb./450 g)**
- **¼ cup/60 g Dijon mustard**
- **2 tsp. dried thyme leaves**
- **1 pkg. (120 g) Stove Top Lower Sodium Stuffing Mix for Chicken**
- **½ cup/125 ml 25%-less-sodium chicken broth**
- **125 g (½ of 250-g pkg.) *Philadelphia* Light Brick Cream Cheese Spread, cubed**
- **2 cups/360 g fresh green beans, steamed**

1. **Heat** oven to 400°F/200°C/mark 6.
2. **Heat** large nonstick skillet on medium heat. Add meat; cook 5 min. or until browned on all sides, turning occasionally. Transfer meat to 13×9-inch baking dish, reserving drippings in skillet. Mix mustard and thyme; spread onto meat.
3. **Bake** 20 to 25 min. or until done (160°F/70°C). Transfer to carving board; tent with foil. Let stand 5 min. Meanwhile, prepare stuffing as directed on package, reducing margarine to 1 Tbsp.
4. **Add** broth to same skillet. Bring to boil on high heat. Add cream cheese spread; cook on medium-low heat 2 min. or until cream cheese is completely melted and sauce is well blended, stirring constantly.
5. **Cut** meat into thin slices. Serve topped with cream cheese sauce along with the stuffing and beans.

note

If you purchased the broth in a 900-ml pkg., store remaining broth in refrigerator up to 1 week. Or, if you purchased a 10-fl. oz./284-ml can, pour the remaining broth into a glass container; store in refrigerator up to 1 week.

Roasted Veggie Sandwich

prep: 5 min. \ total: 17 min. \ makes: 2 servings, 1 sandwich (162 g) each

- **½ red pepper**
- **2 slices red onion (¼ inch thick)**
- **4 slices each yellow squash and zucchini (¼ inch thick)**
- **⅛ tsp. black pepper**
- **2 squares focaccia bread (3 inch), split**
- **¼ cup/60 g *Philadelphia* Spinach Light Cream Cheese Product**

1. **Heat** oven to 400°F/200°C/mark 6.
2. **Make** 2 or 3 small cuts in each short end of red pepper; press pepper to flatten. Place on baking sheet sprayed with cooking spray. Add remaining vegetables. Sprinkle with black pepper.
3. **Bake** 10 to 12 min. or until crisp-tender.
4. **Spread** cut sides of focaccia with cream cheese product; fill with vegetables.

use your barbecue:
Place grill pan on barbecue grate; heat on medium heat. Add vegetables to heated pan; brush with 1 Tbsp. olive oil. Grill 10 min. or until crisp-tender, turning after 5 min.

Three Cheese Chicken Penne Pasta Bake

prep: 20 min. \ total: 43 min. \ makes: 4 servings, 2 cups (500 ml) each

- **1½ cups/180 g multigrain penne pasta, uncooked**
- **1 pkg. (283 g) fresh baby spinach leaves**
- **1 lb. (450 g) boneless skinless chicken breasts, cut into bite-size pieces**
- **1 tsp. dried basil leaves**
- **1½ cups (½ of 700-ml jar) pasta sauce**
- **1⅔ cups (½ of 796-ml can) diced tomatoes, drained**
- **¼ cup/60 g *Philadelphia* Light Cream Cheese Spread**
- **1 cup/120 g Kraft Part Skim Mozzarella Shredded Cheese, divided**
- **2 Tbsp. Kraft 100% Parmesan Light Grated Cheese**

1. **Heat** oven to 375°F/190°C/mark 5. Cook pasta as directed on package, adding spinach to the boiling water for the last 1 min.
2. **Meanwhile,** heat large nonstick skillet sprayed with cooking spray on medium-high heat. Add chicken and basil; cook 3 min. or until chicken is no longer pink, stirring frequently. Add pasta sauce and tomatoes; bring to boil. Reduce heat to low; simmer 3 min. or until chicken is cooked through. Stir in cream cheese spread until melted.
3. **Drain** pasta and spinach; return to same saucepan. Add chicken mixture; mix lightly. Stir in ½ cup/60 g mozzarella cheese. Spoon into 2-L or 8-inch square baking dish.
4. **Bake** 20 min. or until heated through. Sprinkle with remaining mozzarella cheese and the Parmesan cheese. Bake 3 min. or until cheese is melted.

20-Minute Skillet Salmon

prep: 10 min. \ total: 20 min. \ makes: 4 servings

- **2 tsp. oil**
- **4 salmon fillets (1 lb./450 g)**
- **¾ cup/185 ml skim milk**
- **125 g (½ of 250-g tub) *Philadelphia* Herb & Garlic Light Cream Cheese Spread**
- **½ cup/90 g chopped cucumbers**
- **2 Tbsp. chopped fresh dill**

1. **Heat** oil in large skillet on medium-high heat. Add fish; cook 5 min. on each side or until fish flakes easily with fork. Remove from skillet; cover to keep warm.
2. **Add** milk and cream cheese spread to skillet; cook and stir until cream cheese is melted and mixture is well blended. Stir in cucumbers and dill.
3. **Return** fish to skillet; cook 2 min. or until heated through. Serve topped with cream cheese sauce.

special extra

Top salmon with fresh dill sprigs before serving.

Creamy Rosé Penne

prep: 20 min. \ total: 20 min. \ makes: 4 servings, 1¼ cups (300 ml) each

- **3 cups/360 g penne pasta, uncooked**
- **1½ cups/400 g pasta sauce**
- **⅓ cup (⅓ of 250-g tub) *Philadelphia* Cream Cheese Spread**
- **¼ cup/20 g fresh basil**

1. **Cook** pasta as directed on package, omitting salt.
2. **Meanwhile,** heat pasta sauce in nonstick skillet on medium-high heat. Stir in cream cheese spread; cook and stir constantly 2 to 3 min. or until melted.
3. **Drain** pasta; toss with sauce until evenly coated. Top with basil.

Creamy Potato Leek Soup

prep: 20 min. \ total: 1 hour \ makes: 10 servings, 1 cup (250 ml) each

- **2 leeks, cut into 1-inch pieces**
- **2 lb. (900 g) Yukon Gold potatoes (about 4), peeled, cut into ½-inch cubes**
- **2 Tbsp. Kraft Extra Virgin Olive Oil Tuscan Italian Dressing**
- **1 Tbsp. chopped fresh rosemary**
- **3 cups/750 ml water**
- **1 can (284 ml) 25%-less-sodium chicken broth**
- **1 pkg. (250 g) *Philadelphia* Brick Cream Cheese, cubed, divided**

1. **Heat** oven to 400°F/200°C/mark 6.
2. **Combine** vegetables, dressing and rosemary; spread onto baking sheet. Bake 35 to 40 min. or until vegetables are tender and golden brown, stirring occasionally.
3. **Place** water, broth and ¾ cup cream cheese cubes in large saucepan; cook on medium heat 3 min. or until mixture is well blended, stirring frequently with whisk. Stir in vegetables.
4. **Blend** soup, in batches, in blender until smooth. Return to saucepan; bring to boil. Thin soup with additional water, if desired. Serve topped with remaining cream cheese cubes.

special extra

Top with additional chopped fresh rosemary just before serving.

Entrées

Lasagne Bake for Two

prep: 15 min. \ total: 50 min. \ makes: 2 servings, 1¾ cups (425 ml)

- **2 lasagne noodles, uncooked**
- **½ lb. (225 g) extra-lean ground beef**
- **½ cup/90 g chopped onions**
- **1 clove garlic, minced**
- **1 cup (⅓ of 796-ml/28-fl. oz. can) undrained canned diced tomatoes**
- **2 Tbsp. *Philadelphia* Cream Cheese Spread**
- **4 cups/160 g loosely packed baby spinach leaves**
- **½ cup/60 g Kraft 4 Cheese Italiano Shredded Cheese, divided**

1. **Heat** oven to 350°F/180°C/mark 4.
2. **Cook** noodles as directed on package, omitting salt.
3. **Meanwhile,** brown meat with onions and garlic in large nonstick skillet. Add tomatoes and cream cheese spread; cook and stir 2 to 3 min. or until cream cheese is melted and mixture just comes to boil. Add spinach; cook and stir 1 min. Remove from heat. Add ¼ cup/30 g shredded cheese; stir until melted.
4. **Drain** noodles. Spoon ⅓ cup/ spinach mixture into each of 2 (85 ml) ramekins; top with noodle, letting excess noodle extend over rim of ramekin. Top each with ⅓ cup spinach mixture; fold noodle back over dish to cover filling. Repeat until all filling is folded between noodle layers; top with remaining shredded cheese.
5. **Bake** 20 min. or until heated through. Let stand 5 min. before serving.

Creamy Tomato Baked Rigatoni

prep: 20 min. \ total: 55 min. \ makes: 6 servings, 1¼ cups (300 ml) each

- **300 g (⅓ of 900-g pkg.) rigatoni pasta, uncooked**
- **2 cups/320 g pasta sauce**
- **½ cup (½ of 250-g tub) *Philadelphia* Cream Cheese Spread**
- **1 cup/180 g frozen broccoli florets, thawed**
- **1 cup/180 g frozen cauliflower florets, thawed**
- **1 cup/120 g Kraft Part Skim Mozzarella Shredded Cheese, divided**
- **⅓ cup/40 g fresh bread crumbs**
- **2 Tbsp. non-hydrogenated margarine, melted**

1. **Heat** oven to 350°F / 180°C/mark 4.
2. **Cook** pasta as directed on package. Meanwhile, microwave pasta sauce in large microwaveable bowl on HIGH 1½ to 2 min. or until hot. Add cream cheese spread; stir until well blended. Stir in vegetables and ½ cup mozzarella.
3. **Drain** pasta. Add to vegetable mixture; mix lightly. Spoon into 9-inch/23 cm square baking dish sprayed with cooking spray. Combine remaining mozzarella, bread crumbs and margarine; sprinkle over pasta mixture.
4. **Bake** 30 to 35 min. or until casserole is heated through and top is golden brown.

Herb & Garlic Meatballs

prep: 15 min. \ total: 37 min. \ makes: 4 servings, ¼ recipe (385 g) each

- **1 lb. (450 g) extra-lean ground beef**
- **½ cup/65 g dry bread crumbs**
- **½ cup (½ of 250-g tub) *Philadelphia* Herb & Garlic Cream Cheese Spread**
- **2 Tbsp. oil**
- **2 cups/320 g pasta sauce**
- **1 cup/250 ml water**
- **3 cups/420 g hot cooked egg noodles**

1. **Mix** meat, bread crumbs and cream cheese spread until well blended; shape into 24 meatballs, using about 2 Tbsp. for each meatball.
2. **Heat** oil in large nonstick skillet on medium heat. Add meatballs; cook 5 to 6 min. or until evenly browned, turning occasionally. Drain fat from skillet, reserving meatballs in skillet. Add pasta sauce and water to skillet; stir to evenly coat meatballs. Simmer on medium-low heat 10 to 15 min. or until meatballs are done (160°F/ 70°C), stirring frequently.
3. **Serve** over noodles.

how to shape meatballs

For evenly sized meatballs, use small ice cream scoop to portion meat mixture for each meatball.

Florentine Linguine

prep: 30 min. \ total: 30 min. \ makes: 4 servings, 1 cup (250 ml) each

220 g linguine, uncooked

1 Tbsp. olive oil

1 small onion, chopped

1 clove garlic, minced

½ cup (½ of 250-g tub) *Philadelphia* Spinach Light Cream Cheese Product

½ cup/125 ml 25%-less-sodium chicken broth

½ cup/125 ml milk

1. **Cook** pasta as directed on package, omitting salt.
2. **Meanwhile,** heat oil in large nonstick skillet on medium-high heat. Add onions and garlic; cook and stir 5 to 7 min. or until crisp-tender. Add cream cheese product; cook and stir on medium heat 5 min. or until melted. Whisk in broth and milk; cook and stir 2 to 3 min. or until slightly thickened. (Do not boil.)
3. **Drain** pasta. Serve topped with sauce.

Deep-Dish Chicken Pot Pie

prep: 20 min. \ total: 50 min. \ makes: 6 servings, 1/6 recipe (174 g) each

- **1 lb. (450 g) boneless skinless chicken breasts, cut into 1-inch pieces**
- **¼ cup/60 ml Kraft Calorie-Wise Zesty Italian Dressing**
- **125 g (½ of 250-g pkg.) *Philadelphia* Light Brick Cream Cheese Spread, cubed**
- **2 Tbsp. flour**
- **½ cup/125 ml 25%-less-sodium chicken broth**
- **3 cups/550 g frozen mixed vegetables (peas, carrots, corn, green beans), thawed, drained**
- **1 frozen deep-dish pie shell, thawed**

1. **Heat** oven to 375°F/ 190°C/mark 5.
2. **Cook** chicken in dressing in large skillet on medium heat 2 min. Add cream cheese spread; cook and stir 3 to 5 min. or until melted. Stir in flour until well blended. Add broth and vegetables; stir. Simmer 5 min.
3. **Pour** into deep-dish 9-inch/23 cm pie plate. Invert pie shell over filling; flute edge. Cut slits in shell to permit steam to escape.
4. **Bake** 30 min. or until golden brown.

substitute

If a deep-dish pie plate is not available, use a 2-L round casserole instead.

Bacon & Tomato Presto Pasta

prep: 5 min. \ total: 20 min. \ makes: 8 servings, ⅛ recipe (190 g) each

- **8 slices bacon, chopped**
- **1 tub (250 g) *Philadelphia* Herb & Garlic Cream Cheese Spread**
- **1 cup/250 ml milk**
- **½ cup/55 g Kraft 100% Parmesan Grated Cheese**
- **½ cup/90 g cherry tomatoes**
- **6 cups/850 g hot cooked penne pasta**

1. **Cook** bacon in large skillet until crisp, stirring occasionally. Drain bacon; return to skillet.
2. **Add** cream cheese spread, milk, Parmesan and tomatoes; cook on medium-low heat until cream cheese is completely melted and sauce is heated through, stirring frequently.
3. **Stir** in pasta.

special extra

Top with chopped fresh basil or parsley.

Creamy Beef Stroganoff

prep: 10 min. \ total: 50 min. \ makes: 4 servings, ¼ recipe (391 g) each

1 beef flank steak (1 lb./450 g)

1 Tbsp. non-hydrogenated margarine

1 small onion, chopped

1 lb. (450 g) sliced fresh mushrooms

2 bay leaves

1 tsp. chopped fresh thyme

1 can (284 ml) 25%-less-sodium beef broth

½ cup (½ of 250-g tub) *Philadelphia* Cream Cheese Spread

¼ cup/10 g chopped fresh parsley

340 g hot cooked egg noodles

1. **Cook** steak in large skillet on high heat 2 min. on each side or until browned on both sides. Remove from skillet; cover to keep warm.
2. **Add** margarine and onions to skillet; cook on medium heat 5 min. or until onions are crisp-tender, stirring occasionally. Stir in mushrooms, bay leaves and thyme; cook 10 min., stirring occasionally. Add broth; bring to boil. Simmer on low heat 3 min. or until slightly thickened. Add cream cheese spread; cook until melted, stirring frequently. Remove and discard bay leaves.
3. **Cut** steak across the grain into thin slices. Add to skillet; cook 3 to 5 min. or until meat is done. Stir in parsley. Serve over noodles.

variation

Serve over hot cooked rice or mashed potatoes instead of the noodles.

Quick & Creamy Chicken Stew

prep: 10 min. \ total: 26 min. \ makes: 4 servings, 1½ cups (375 ml) each

- **¾ lb. (340 g) small red potatoes (about 8), quartered**
- **2 Tbsp. water**
- **1 Tbsp. oil**
- **1 lb. (450 g) boneless skinless chicken breasts, cut into bite-size pieces**
- **1 can (10 fl. oz./284 ml) reduced-fat condensed cream of chicken soup**
- **¼ cup/60 ml Kraft Calorie-Wise Zesty Italian Dressing**
- **2 cups/360 g frozen peas and carrots**
- **½ cup (½ of 250-g tub) *Philadelphia* Herb & Garlic Light Cream Cheese Spread**

1. **Place** potatoes in microwaveable dish. Add water; cover with lid. Microwave on HIGH 7 min. or until potatoes are tender. Meanwhile, heat oil in large saucepan on medium-high heat. Add chicken; cook 7 min. or until evenly browned, stirring occasionally.
2. **Add** potatoes, soup, dressing and frozen vegetables to saucepan. Bring to boil; cover. Simmer on medium-low heat 3 min. or until chicken is done (170°F/77°C), and vegetables are heated through.
3. **Stir** in cream cheese spread; cook 3 min. or until melted, stirring occasionally.

Sausage & Peppers Lasagne

prep: 30 min. \ total: 1 hour 30 min. \ makes: 12 servings, 1 piece (208 g) each

- **½ lb. (225 g) Italian sausage**
- **1 onion, chopped**
- **½ cup/90 g each chopped green and red peppers**
- **2 pkg. (250 g each) *Philadelphia* Brick Cream Cheese, softened**
- **½ cup/125 ml milk**
- **2½ cups/300 g shredded mozzarella cheese**
- **½ cup/55 g grated Parmesan cheese**
- **2½ cups/650 g spaghetti sauce**
- **½ tsp. dried oregano leaves**
- **½ cup/125 ml water**
- **12 lasagne noodles, cooked**

1. **Heat** oven to 350°F/180°C/mark 4.
2. **Brown** sausage with vegetables in large skillet. Meanwhile, beat cream cheese and milk in medium bowl with mixer until well blended. Combine mozzarella and Parmesan. Reserve 1½ cups/85 g. Add remaining to cream cheese mixture; mix well.
3. **Drain** sausage mixture; return to skillet. Stir in spaghetti sauce, oregano and water. Spread ⅓ of the meat sauce onto bottom of 13×9-inch/33×23 cm baking dish; top with 3 noodles, half the cream cheese mixture, 3 more noodles and half the remaining meat sauce. Top with 3 more noodles, then layers of remaining cream cheese mixture, noodles and meat sauce. Sprinkle with reserved cheese mixture; cover.
4. **Bake** 1 hour or until heated through, uncovering after 45 min. Let stand 15 min. before cutting to serve.

variation:

Substitute extra-lean ground beef for the sausage and 1 thawed 300 g. pkg. frozen chopped spinach for the peppers. Squeeze spinach to remove excess liquid before adding to cooked ground beef and onions with the spaghetti sauce and oregano.

Creamy Pasta Primavera

prep: 25 min. \ total: 25 min. \ makes: 6 servings, 2 cups (500 ml) each

- **4 cups/480 g whole grain penne pasta, uncooked**
- **2 Tbsp. Kraft Calorie-Wise Zesty Italian Dressing**
- **1½ lb. (675 g) boneless skinless chicken breasts, cut into 1-inch pieces**
- **2 zucchini, cut into bite-size chunks**
- **1½ cups/270 g cut-up fresh asparagus (1-inch lengths)**
- **1 red pepper, chopped**
- **1 cup/250 ml 25%-less-sodium chicken broth**
- **½ cup (½ of 250-g tub) *Philadelphia* Light Cream Cheese Spread**
- **¼ cup/55 g Kraft 100% Parmesan Light Grated Cheese**

1. **Cook** pasta in Dutch oven or large saucepan as directed on package.
2. **Meanwhile,** heat dressing in large skillet on medium heat. Add chicken and vegetables; cook 10 to 12 min. or until chicken is done (170°F/77°C), stirring frequently. Add broth and cream cheese spread; cook 2 min. or until cream cheese is melted, stirring constantly. Stir in Parmesan.
3. **Drain** pasta; return to pan. Add chicken mixture; mix lightly. Cook 1 min. or until heated through.

Creamy Chicken, Bacon & Tomato Pasta

prep: 10 min. \ total: 25 min. \ makes: 4 servings, 1¾ cups (425 ml) each

- **3 cups/360 g whole wheat farfalle (bow-tie pasta), uncooked**
- **1 lb. (450 g) boneless skinless chicken breasts, cut into bite-size pieces**
- **3 slices bacon, cooked, crumbled**
- **1 can (19 fl. oz./540 ml) Italian-style diced tomatoes, undrained**
- **125 g (½ of 250-g pkg.) *Philadelphia* Light Brick Cream Cheese Spread, cubed**
- **½ cup/125 ml water**
- **¼ tsp. black pepper**
- **3 Tbsp. Kraft 100% Parmesan Light Grated Cheese**

1. **Cook** pasta as directed on package.
2. **Meanwhile,** cook chicken in large skillet on medium heat 5 to 6 min. or until chicken is done (170°F/77°C), stirring occasionally. Add next 5 ingredients; mix well. Cook 3 min. or until cream cheese spread is completely melted and mixture is well blended, stirring frequently.
3. **Drain** pasta; place in large bowl. Add sauce; mix lightly. Sprinkle with Parmesan.

Pork Medallions Alfredo

prep: 10 min. \ total: 20 min. \ makes: 4 servings, ¼ recipe (188 g) each

- **1 pork tenderloin (1 lb./450 g), cut into ½-inch-thick slices**
- **½ cup (½ of 250-g tub) *Philadelphia* Herb & Garlic Cream Cheese Spread**
- **⅓ cup/85 ml 25%-less-sodium chicken broth**
- **¼ cup/60 ml Kraft Signature Balsamic Vinaigrette Dressing**
- **¼ cup/25 g Kraft 100% Parmesan Grated Cheese**
- **1 Tbsp. lemon juice**
- **2 Tbsp. fresh basil, chopped**

1 **Heat** large nonstick skillet sprayed with cooking spray on medium-high heat. Add meat; cook 2 min. on each side or until lightly browned on both sides.

2 **Add** all remaining ingredients except basil; cook 6 min. or until cream cheese spread is melted, sauce is thickened and meat is done, stirring frequently.

3 **Sprinkle** with basil.

serving suggestion

Serve with cooked egg noodles and peas.

Linguine with Silky Mushroom Sauce

prep: 5 min. \ total: 20 min. \ makes: 4 servings, 1¼ cups (300 ml) each

225 g (¼ of 900-g pkg.) linguine, uncooked

½ lb. (225 g) sliced fresh mushrooms

½ cup/125 ml 25%-less-sodium chicken broth

½ cup (½ of 250-g tub) *Philadelphia* Chive & Onion Light Cream Cheese Product

2 cups/80 g baby spinach leaves

2 Tbsp. Kraft 100% Parmesan Light Grated Cheese

Black pepper

1 **Cook** pasta as directed on package.

2 **Meanwhile,** heat skillet sprayed with cooking spray on medium-high heat. Add mushrooms; cook and stir 8 min. or until lightly browned. Add broth and cream cheese product; mix well. Add spinach; cook until just wilted.

3 **Drain** pasta; toss with sauce. Sprinkle with Parmesan cheese and pepper.

shortcut

Packaged sliced fresh mushrooms are available in the produce department of your grocery store.

Asparagus Bow-Tie Pasta

prep: 5 min. \ total: 28 min. \ makes: 4 servings, 1 cup (250 ml) each

2 cups/240 g farfalle (bow-tie pasta), uncooked

1 lb. (450 g) fresh asparagus spears, trimmed, cut into 1-inch lengths

½ cup/90 g halved orange pepper strips

¼ cup/90 g julienne-cut oil-packed sun-dried tomatoes, undrained

½ cup/125 ml 25%-less-sodium chicken broth

50 g (⅕ of 250-g pkg.) *Philadelphia* Brick Cream Cheese, cubed

1 Tbsp. chopped fresh oregano

1 cup/120 g Kraft 4 Cheese Italiano Shredded Cheese

1 **Cook** pasta in large saucepan as directed on package, omitting salt and adding asparagus to boiling water for the last 2 min. Drain.

2 **Meanwhile,** cook peppers and tomatoes in large skillet on medium-high heat 2 to 3 min. or until crisp-tender, stirring frequently.

3 **Add** pasta mixture, broth, cream cheese and oregano to skillet; mix well. Cook and stir 5 min. or until sauce is slightly thickened. Top with shredded cheese; cook 2 to 3 min. or until cheese begins to melt.

special extra

Add 1½ cups/480 g cooked cleaned shrimp or chopped cooked chicken to skillet with the cooked pasta.

Fish in Roasted Red Pepper Sauce

prep: 10 min. \ total: 30 min. \ makes: 4 servings, ¼ recipe (147 g) each

- **4 tilapia fillets (1 lb./450 g)**
- **¼ cup/35 g flour**
- **¼ cup/60 ml Italian dressing**
- **½ cup/90 g sliced onions**
- **60 g (about ¼ of 250-g pkg.) *Philadelphia* Brick Cream Cheese, softened**
- **¼ cup/45 g roasted fresh red peppers**
- **¼ cup/60 ml chicken broth**
- **1 clove garlic**
- **2 Tbsp. chopped fresh cilantro**

1. **Coat** both sides of fish fillets with flour. Heat dressing in large skillet on medium-high heat. Add onions; cook and stir 5 min. or until crisp-tender. Add fish; cook 5 to 7 min. on each side or until fish flakes easily with fork.
2. **Meanwhile,** blend cream cheese, red peppers, broth and garlic in blender until smooth; pour into saucepan. Bring to boil on medium-high heat, stirring frequently; simmer on low heat 5 min., stirring occasionally.
3. **Serve** fish topped with cream cheese sauce and cilantro.

substitute:

Substitute jarred roasted red peppers or roasted poblano peppers for the roasted fresh red peppers.

Curry with Pork & Peppers

prep: 10 min. \ total: 32 min. \ makes: 4 servings, 1¼ cups (300 ml) each

- **1 lb. (450 g) pork tenderloin, cut into 1-inch pieces**
- **1 onion, cut into 1-inch pieces**
- **1 red pepper, cut into 1-inch pieces**
- **1 green pepper, cut into 1-inch pieces**
- **½ cup (½ of 250-g tub) *Philadelphia* Cream Cheese Spread**
- **1 Tbsp. Thai yellow curry paste**
- **½ cup/125 ml coconut milk**
- **½ cup/125 ml water**
- **2 cups cooked rice**
- **¼ cup/10 g chopped cilantro (optional)**

1. **Heat** large skillet sprayed with cooking spray on medium-high heat. Add meat; cook and stir 4 min. or until evenly browned. Add vegetables; cook 4 to 6 min. or until vegetables are crisp-tender, stirring constantly.
2. **Add** cream cheese spread, curry paste, coconut milk and water; cook until cream cheese is melted, stirring constantly. Bring just to boil; simmer on medium-low heat 8 to 10 min. or until meat is cooked through, stirring frequently.
3. **Serve** over rice; top with cilantro, if desired.

special extra

Top with ¼ cup/20 g toasted shredded coconut just before serving.

Mediterranean-Style Stuffed Chicken

prep: 20 min. \ total: 1 hour \ makes: 4 servings, ¼ recipe (151 g) each

- **125 g (½ of 250-g pkg.) Philadelphia Light Brick Cream Cheese Spread, softened**
- **3 slices bacon, cooked, crumbled**
- **2 Tbsp. dry bread crumbs**
- **2 Tbsp. chopped kalamata olives**
- **2 Tbsp. coarsely chopped slivered almonds**
- **1 egg**
- **1 Tbsp. plus 1 tsp. chopped fresh thyme, divided**
- **4 small boneless skinless chicken breasts (1 lb./450 g)**
- **2 tsp. oil**
- **½ cup/125 ml dry white wine**
- **½ cup/125 ml 25%-less-sodium chicken broth**

1. **Heat** oven to 325°F/160°C/mark 3.
2. **Combine** first 6 ingredients. Add 1 Tbsp. thyme; mix well. Use small sharp knife to cut pocket in thick long side of each chicken breast, being careful to not cut through to opposite side. Fill pockets with cream cheese mixture.
3. **Heat** oil in large skillet on medium-high heat. Add chicken; cook 3 to 4 min. on each side or until browned on both sides. Transfer to 13×9-inch/33×23 cm baking dish sprayed with cooking spray; cover. Reserve drippings in skillet.
4. **Bake** 25 to 30 min. or until chicken is done (170°F/77°C). Meanwhile, add wine and broth to drippings; cook on medium heat 10 min. or until liquid is reduced by half, stirring frequently to scrape up browned bits from bottom of skillet. Stir in remaining thyme.
5. **Slice** chicken. Serve topped with sauce.

serving suggestion:
Serve with roasted butternut squash and broccoli.

Fisherman's Chowder

prep: 10 min. \ total: 50 min. \ makes: 8 servings, 1 cup (250 ml) each

- **6 slices bacon, chopped**
- **1 large onion, chopped**
- **2 stalks celery, chopped**
- **1 large carrot, chopped**
- **2 cups /500 ml25%-less-sodium chicken broth**
- **1 large potato, diced**
- **½ cup (½ of 250-g tub) *Philadelphia* Cream Cheese Spread**
- **2 cups/500 ml milk**
- **1 pkg. (400 g) frozen cod fillets, thawed, drained and cut into 2-inch pieces**

1. **Cook** bacon in large saucepan until crisp, stirring occasionally. Use slotted spoon to remove bacon from pan, reserving 1 Tbsp. drippings in pan. Drain bacon on paper towels.
2. **Add** next 3 ingredients to drippings in pan; cook on medium heat 12 to 14 min. or until vegetables are crisp-tender, stirring occasionally. Add broth and potatoes; bring to boil. Cover; simmer 10 to 12 min. or until potatoes are tender.
3. **Add** cream cheese spread; cook, uncovered, 2 to 3 min. or until melted, stirring frequently. Add milk, fish and bacon; stir. Bring to boil, stirring frequently. Cook 3 to 4 min. or until fish flakes easily with fork.

Mozzarella-Stuffed Chicken Breasts

prep: 15 min. \ total: 50 min. \ makes: 4 servings, 1 stuffed chicken breast (215 g) each

- **63 g (¼ of 250-g pkg.) *Philadelphia* Light Brick Cream Cheese Spread, softened**
- **¼ cup/45 g finely chopped green peppers**
- **½ tsp. dried oregano leaves**
- **¼ tsp. garlic salt**
- **1 cup/120 g Kraft Part Skim Mozzarella Shredded Cheese, divided**
- **4 small boneless skinless chicken breasts (1 lb./450 g), pounded to ¼-inch thickness**
- **1 cup/260 g pasta sauce**

1. **Heat** oven to 400°F/ 200°C/mark 6.
2. **Mix** first 4 ingredients until well blended; stir in ½ cup/60 g mozzarella.
3. **Place** chicken, top-sides down, on work surface; spread with cheese mixture. Starting at one short end, tightly roll up each breast; place, seam-side down, in 8-inch/20 cm square baking dish sprayed with cooking spray. Spoon pasta sauce over chicken; cover.
4. **Bake** 30 min. or until chicken is done (170°F/77°C). Sprinkle with remaining mozzarella; bake, uncovered, 3 to 5 min. or until melted.

Greek Chicken with Tzatziki Sauce

prep: 15 min. \ total: 45 min. \ makes: 4 servings, 2 kabobs (99 g) and 2 Tbsp. (30 ml) sauce each

- **½ cup (½ of 250-g tub) *Philadelphia* Dill Cream Cheese Product**
- **6 Tbsp. milk**
- **1 Tbsp. lemon juice**
- **1 green onion, chopped**
- **1 clove garlic, minced**
- **1 lb. (450 g) boneless skinless chicken breasts, cut into bite-size pieces**
- **¼ cup/45 g finely chopped English cucumbers**

1. **Whisk** first 5 ingredients until well blended. Pour half over chicken in medium bowl; stir to evenly coat. Stir cucumbers into remaining sauce. Refrigerate both 20 min.
2. **Heat** barbecue to medium-high heat. Remove chicken from marinade; discard marinade. Thread chicken onto 8 skewers. Grill 8 to 10 min. or until done (170°F/ 77°C), turning occasionally.
3. **Serve** with tzatziki sauce.

serving suggestion

Serve with hot cooked whole grains and your favourite vegetables.

Creamy Shrimp Linguine

prep: 10 min. \ total: 25 min. \ makes: 4 servings, 1½ cups (375 ml) each

- **220 g linguine, uncooked**
- **1 Tbsp. oil**
- **1 lb. (450 g) uncooked deveined peeled large shrimp**
- **2 cloves garlic, minced**
- **½ cup (½ of 250-g tub) *Philadelphia* Dill Cream Cheese Product**
- **¾ cup/185 ml 25%-less-sodium chicken broth**
- **1 Tbsp. lemon zest**
- **2 cups/360 g snow peas, halved**
- **1 cup/180 g cherry tomatoes, halved**

1. **Cook** pasta as directed on package, omitting salt.
2. **Meanwhile,** heat oil in large nonstick skillet on medium-high heat. Add shrimp and garlic; cook and stir 3 to 5 min. or until shrimp turn pink. Remove from heat; cover to keep warm.
3. **Add** cream cheese product, broth and zest; cook and stir 2 to 3 min. or until cream cheese is melted and sauce is well blended. Add shrimp, snow peas and tomatoes; cook and stir 3 min. or until heated through.
4. **Drain** pasta. Add to shrimp mixture; toss to coat.

Side Dishes

Mixed Green Salad with Warm Cream Cheese “Croutons”

prep: 15 min. \ total: 15 min. \ makes: 8 servings, 3 “croutons” each

- **125 g (½ of 250-g pkg.) *Philadelphia* Brick Cream Cheese, cut into ½-inch cubes**
- **¼ cup/30 g finely chopped almonds**
- **8 cups/320 g torn salad greens**
- **1 Granny Smith apple, thinly sliced**
- **½ cup/120 g pomegranate seeds**
- **⅓ cup/80 ml Kraft Signature Balsamic Vinaigrette Dressing**

1. **Spray** large skillet with cooking spray; heat on medium heat. Meanwhile, coat cream cheese cubes with almonds.
2. **Add** to skillet; cook 3 min. or until golden brown, turning occasionally.
3. **Toss** remaining ingredients in large bowl. Top with cheese. Serve immediately.

Creamy Spinach

prep: 5 min. \ total: 18 min. \ makes: 4 servings, ⅔ cup (150 ml) each

- **1 tsp. oil**
- **½ small red onion, sliced**
- **125 g (½ of 250-g pkg.) *Philadelphia* Light Brick Cream Cheese Spread, cubed**
- **1 Tbsp. skim milk**
- **¼ tsp. black pepper**
- **2 pkg. (142 g each) baby spinach leaves**

1 **Heat** oil in medium saucepan on medium-high heat. Add onions; cook and stir 3 to 4 min. or until crisp-tender.

2 **Stir** in cream cheese spread, milk and pepper; cook on low heat 1 to 2 min. or until cream cheese is melted and sauce is well blended.

3 **Add** ⅓ of the spinach; cook 2 min. or just until wilted, stirring frequently. Add remaining spinach, in batches, cooking and stirring 1 to 2 min. after each addition just until wilted.

special extra:

Cook ½ cup/60 g sliced fresh mushrooms with the onions.

Creamy Lemon Asparagus Risotto

prep: 10 min. \ total: 20 min. \ makes: 6 servings

- **2 Tbsp. olive oil**
- **1 medium onion, finely chopped**
- **2 cups/300 g instant white rice, uncooked**
- **½ lb./225 g asparagus, cut into 1-inch pieces**
- **2 cups/500 ml chicken broth**
- **2 Tbsp. *Philadelphia* Light Cream Cheese Spread**
- **Grated zest and juice of 1 lemon**

1. **Heat** oil in large skillet on medium heat. Add onions; cook and stir 2 min. or until tender.
2. **Stir** in rice, asparagus and broth. Bring to boil. Reduce heat to low; simmer 5 min.
3. **Add** cream cheese spread, zest and juice; stir until well blended.

serving suggestions

Serve this risotto with grilled chicken or shrimp.

Butternut Squash Puff

prep: 10 min. \ total: 40 min. \ makes: 4 servings

- **2 cups/320 g mashed cooked butternut squash**
- **½ cup/120 g *Philadelphia* Light Cream Cheese Spread**
- **¾ cup/90 g dry bread crumbs, divided**
- **2 Tbsp. packed brown sugar**
- **1 egg**
- **Dash each of ground ginger, black pepper and salt**

1. **Combine** butternut squash with cream cheese spread, ½ cup/60 g dry bread crumbs, brown sugar, egg and a dash each of ground ginger, pepper and salt.
2. **Place** in a greased shallow baking dish (1 L). Sprinkle with additional ¼ cup/30 g bread crumbs.
3. **Bake** at 350°F/180°C/mark 4 for 30 min. or until lightly browned.

Bacon & Maple Scalloped Potatoes

prep: 15 min. \ total: 1 hour 30 min. \ makes: 8 servings, 1 cup (250 ml) each

- **1 red onion, thinly sliced**
- **125 g (½ of 250-g pkg.) *Philadelphia* Brick Cream Cheese, cubed**
- **1 can (10 fl. oz./284 ml) 25%-less-sodium chicken broth**
- **½ cup/125 ml milk**
- **¼ cup/30 g Oscar Mayer Real Bacon Recipe Pieces**
- **¼ cup/60 ml maple syrup**
- **2 lb. (900 g) Yukon Gold potatoes (about 6), cut into ¼-inch-thick slices**
- **1 cup/120 g Kraft Double Cheddar Shredded Cheese**

1. **Heat** oven to 400°F/ 200°C/mark 6.
2. **Cook** onions in a large skillet sprayed with cooking spray on medium-high heat 3 to 5 min. or until crisp-tender, stirring frequently. Remove onions from skillet.
3. **Add** cream cheese, broth and milk to skillet; cook and stir on medium-low heat 5 min. or until cream cheese is melted and mixture is well blended. Remove from heat; stir in bacon and syrup.
4. **Place** half the potatoes in 13×9-inch/ 33×23cm baking dish sprayed with cooking spray; cover with layers of onions and shredded cheese. Top with remaining potatoes and cream cheese sauce; cover.
5. **Bake** 1 hour 5 min. or until potatoes are tender and top is golden brown, uncovering after 50 min.

Creamy Vegetable Orzo

prep: 10 min. \ total: 35 min. \ makes: 6 servings, ½ cup (125 ml) each

- **1 Tbsp. oil**
- **1 small onion, chopped**
- **½ cup/90 g each chopped green and red peppers**
- **1 cup/180 g frozen corn**
- **¾ cup/90 g orzo pasta, uncooked**
- **1¾ cups/435 ml 25%-less-sodium chicken broth**
- **½ cup (½ of 250-g tub) *Philadelphia* Sundried Tomato & Basil Light Cream Cheese Product**

1. **Heat** oil in large skillet on medium heat. Add onions; cook 4 min., stirring frequently. Stir in peppers and corn; cook and stir 2 min. Add orzo; cook and stir 1 min.
2. **Stir** in broth; bring to boil on high heat. Simmer on medium-low heat 10 to 12 min. or until orzo and vegetables are tender and most of the liquid is absorbed, stirring occasionally.
3. **Add** cream cheese product; cook 1 to 2 min. or until cream cheese is melted and sauce is well blended, stirring constantly.

special extra

Add 1 Tbsp. chopped fresh herbs, such as basil or rosemary, to the cooked vegetables with the broth.

Roasted Sweet Potato & Carrot Purée

prep: 15 min. \ total: 1 hour 20 min. \ makes: 6 servings, ½ cup (125 ml) each

- **1 lb. (450 g) sweet potatoes (about 3), peeled, cut into ½-inch pieces**
- **8 carrots (about 1 lb./450 g), peeled, cut into ½-inch slices**
- **3 Tbsp. olive oil**
- **2 Tbsp. packed brown sugar**
- **1 tsp. salt**
- **1½ cups/375 ml 25%-less-sodium chicken broth, divided**
- **125 g (½ of 250-g pkg.) *Philadelphia* Brick Cream Cheese, cubed**

1. **Heat** oven to 375°F/ 190°C/mark 5.
2. **Combine** first 5 ingredients; spread onto bottom of 17×11½×¾-inch/42.5×30×2cm pan. Pour 1 cup broth over vegetable mixture.
3. **Bake** 45 to 55 min. or until broth is absorbed and vegetables are tender and caramelized, stirring occasionally.
4. **Spoon** vegetables into food processor. Add remaining broth and cream cheese; process until smooth. Return to pan; cook 10 min. or until heated through, stirring frequently.

special extra

Before processing roasted vegetables in food processor, reserve ½ cup/90 g of the vegetables to use as a garnish for the finished dish.

Creamy Citrus & Herb Asparagus

prep: 10 min. \ total: 10 min. \ makes: 6 servings, ⅙ recipe (108 g) each

- **2 lb. (900 g) fresh asparagus spears, trimmed**
- **1 Tbsp. water**
- **¼ cup/60 ml 25%-less-sodium chicken broth**
- **½ cup (½ of 250-g tub) *Philadelphia* Herb & Garlic Light Cream Cheese Spread**
- **1 tsp. lemon zest**

1. **Place** asparagus in microwaveable casserole dish. Add water; cover with waxed paper. Microwave on HIGH 4 to 5 min. or until asparagus is crisp-tender.
2. **Meanwhile,** heat broth in small saucepan. Add cream cheese spread; cook until cream cheese is melted and sauce is slightly thickened, stirring constantly. Stir in zest.
3. **Drain** asparagus; top with sauce.

serving suggestion:

For a simple and elegant presentation, divide cooked asparagus spears into 6 bundles; tie each with a steamed green onion.

Creamy Double-Mashed Potatoes

prep: 15 min. \ total: 35 min. \ makes: 6 servings, ¾ cup (175 ml) each

- **1 lb. (450 g) sweet potatoes (about 3), peeled, cut into chunks**
- **1 lb. (450 g) red potatoes (about 3), peeled, cut into chunks**
- **¼ cup/60 g Philadelphia Light Cream Cheese Spread**
- **½ cup/125 ml 25%-less-sodium chicken broth**
- **4 slices bacon, cooked, crumbled**

1. **Cook** potatoes in boiling water in large saucepan 15 to 20 min. or until tender; drain. Return potatoes to pan.
2. **Add** cream cheese spread; mash potatoes just until cream cheese is blended. Gradually add broth, continuing to mash potatoes until of desired consistency.
3. **Stir** in bacon.

substitute

Prepare using Yukon Gold potatoes.

Fabulous Potatoes

prep: 20 min. \ total: 50 min. \ makes: 6 servings

- **2 lb. (900 g) russet potatoes (about 6), peeled, cubed**
- **1 pkg. (250 g) *Philadelphia* Brick Cream Cheese, cubed**
- **1 cup/250 g sour cream**
- **2 green onions, chopped**

1. **Heat** oven to 350°F/ 180°C/mark 4. Add potatoes to boiling water in saucepan; cook until tender. Drain.
2. **Mash** potatoes. Add cream cheese and sour cream; mash until fluffy. Spoon into greased 1.4-L casserole dish; cover.
3. **Bake** 30 min. or until heated through. Top with onions.

use your microwave

Mix all ingredients except onions as directed. Spoon into greased microwaveable 1.4-L casserole dish. Microwave on HIGH 8 to 10 min. or until heated through, stirring after 5 min. Top with onions.

Crust-Topped Broccoli-Cheese Bake

prep: 10 min. \ total: 40 min. \ makes: 14 servings, 1 cup (250 ml) each

- **½ cup (½ of 250-g tub) *Philadelphia* Herb & Garlic Cream Cheese Spread**
- **1 can (10 fl. oz./284 ml) condensed cream of mushroom soup**
- **½ cup/125 ml water**
- **1 pkg. (1 kg) frozen broccoli florets, thawed, drained**
- **1 cup/120 g Kraft Double Cheddar Shredded Cheese**
- **1 sheet (½ of 397-g pkg.) frozen puff pastry, thawed**
- **1 egg, beaten**

1. **Heat** oven to 400°F/ 200°C/mark 6.
2. **Mix** cream cheese spread, soup and water in medium bowl until well blended. Stir in broccoli and Cheddar; spoon into 2½- to 3-L shallow rectangular or oval baking dish.
3. **Roll** out pastry on lightly floured surface to fit baking dish; place over filling in baking dish. Press pastry onto rim of dish to seal; brush lightly with egg. Cut slits in pastry to vent.
4. **Bake** 30 min. or until filling is heated through and pastry is puffed and golden brown.

Twice-Baked Sweet Potatoes

prep: 10 min. \ total: 53 min. \ makes: 4 servings

- **2 large sweet potatoes (1½ lb./680 g)**
- **¼ cup/60 g *Philadelphia* Light Cream Cheese Spread**
- **2 Tbsp. skim milk**
- **1 Tbsp. packed brown sugar**
- **¼ tsp. ground cinnamon**
- **¼ cup/ 30g chopped pecans**

1. **Heat** oven to 425°F/220°C/mark 7.
2. **Cut** potatoes lengthwise in half; place, cut-sides down, in foil-lined 15×10×1-inch/ 30×25×2 cm pan. Bake 30 to 35 min. or until tender.
3. **Scoop** out centres of potatoes into bowl, leaving ¼-inch/6 mm-thick shells. Add cream cheese spread, milk, sugar and cinnamon to potatoes; mash until blended.
4. **Fill** shells with potato mixture; top with nuts. Bake 8 min. or until potatoes are heated through and nuts are toasted.

Crowd-Pleasing Scalloped Potatoes

prep: 30 min. \ total: 2 hours \ makes: 18 servings, ½ cup (125 ml) each

- **1 tub (250 g) *Philadelphia* Herb & Garlic Cream Cheese Spread**
- **2 cups/500 ml 25%-less-sodium chicken broth**
- **1 cup/250 ml milk**
- **⅔ cup/80 g Oscar Mayer Real Bacon Bits, divided**
- **4½ lb. (2 kg) Yukon Gold potatoes (about 12), cut into ¼-inch-thick slices**
- **1 onion, thinly sliced**
- **1 cup/120 g Kraft Mozza-Cheddar Shredded Cheese**

1. **Heat** oven to 400°F/200°C/mark 6.
2. **Cook** cream cheese spread, broth and milk in saucepan on medium heat until cream cheese is melted and mixture comes to boil, stirring constantly with whisk.
3. **Reserve** 2 Tbsp. bacon bits. Layer half each of the potatoes, onions and remaining bacon bits in 13×9-inch/33×23cm baking dish; repeat layers. Add cream cheese sauce; cover.
4. **Bake** 1 hour 30 min. or until potatoes are tender and top is golden brown, uncovering and topping with shredded cheese and reserved bacon bits the last 10 min.

shortcut

Skip the onions and use *Philadelphia* Chive & Onion Cream Cheese Product instead.

Easy Carrot & Broccoli au Gratin

prep: 10 min. \ total: 25 min. \ makes: 8 servings

- **2 cups/360 g baby carrots, cut in half**
- **1 bunch broccoli, cut into florets (about 4 cups/720 g)**
- **10 Ritz Crackers, crushed**
- **3 Tbsp. Kraft 100% Parmesan Grated Cheese**
- **1 Tbsp. non-hydrogenated margarine, melted**
- **½ cup/125 g Cheez Whiz Cheese Spread**
- **¼ cup (¼ of 250-g tub) *Philadelphia* Cream Cheese Spread**

1. **Bring** 3 cups/750 ml water to boil in large saucepan on medium-high heat. Add carrots. Reduce heat to medium-low; simmer 8 min. Add broccoli; simmer an additional 3 min. or until vegetables are crisp-tender. Meanwhile, mix cracker crumbs, Parmesan cheese and margarine; set aside.
2. **Microwave** Cheez Whiz and cream cheese spread in 2-cup microwaveable measuring cup or medium bowl on HIGH 1 min.; stir. Microwave an additional 30 sec. or until Cheez Whiz and cream cheese are completely melted and mixture is well blended when stirred.
3. **Drain** vegetables; place in serving bowl. Top with cheese sauce; sprinkle with crumb mixture.

shortcut

Look for ¾ lb./340 g packages of fresh broccoli florets in the produce section of your supermarket. Each bag contains about 4 cups which is just the amount you need to prepare this tasty recipe.

Lemon & Parsley Baby Carrots

prep: 5 min. \ total: 40 min. \ makes: 4 servings, ⅔ cup (150 ml) each

- **1 pkg. (1 lb./450 g) baby carrots**
- **1 cup/250 ml water**
- **⅓ cup/85 ml 25%-less-sodium chicken broth**
- **125 g (½ of 250-g pkg.) *Philadelphia* Brick Cream Cheese, cubed**
- **1 tsp. lemon zest**
- **1 Tbsp. chopped fresh parsley**

1. **Bring** carrots and water to boil in medium saucepan on medium-high heat; cover. Cook 6 to 8 min. or until carrots are crisp-tender. Use slotted spoon to transfer carrots to bowl; reserve water in pan.
2. **Return** water to boil; cook 6 to 8 min. or until reduced by half. Add broth, cream cheese and zest; stir. Simmer on low heat 2 to 3 min. or until cream cheese is melted and sauce is well blended, stirring frequently. Stir in parsley.
3. **Add** carrots; toss to coat.

Creamy Tomato-Chicken Risotto

prep: 10 min. \ total: 43 min. \ makes: 8 servings, 1¼ cups (300 ml) each

- **½ cup (½ of 250-g tub) *Philadelphia* Light Cream Cheese Spread**
- **1 can (28 fl. oz. /796 ml) diced tomatoes, drained, divided**
- **⅓ cup/80 ml Kraft Calorie-Wise Zesty Italian Dressing, divided**
- **2 lb. (900 g) boneless skinless chicken breasts, cut into bite-size pieces**
- **1 onion, chopped**
- **2 carrots, chopped**
- **1½ cups/225 g long-grain white rice, uncooked**
- **5½ cups/625 ml hot water, divided**

1. **Blend** cream cheese spread and half the tomatoes in blender until smooth. Heat ¼ cup dressing in large skillet on medium heat. Add chicken; cook 6 min. or until done (170°F/77°C), stirring occasionally. Remove from skillet; cover to keep warm.
2. **Cook** onions, carrots and rice in remaining dressing in same skillet 3 min. or until rice is opaque, stirring frequently. Gradually add 1½ cups/375 ml of the water; cook 5 min. or until water is completely absorbed, stirring occasionally. Repeat with the remaining water in batches, returning chicken to skillet with the last addition of water.
3. **Stir** in cream cheese mixture and remaining tomatoes; cook 3 min. or until heated through, stirring occasionally.

special extra

Sprinkle with chopped fresh parsley just before serving.

BLT Bruschetta

prep: 20 min. \ total: 24 min. \ makes: 18 servings, 2 bruschetta (32 g) each

- **1 French bread baguette (20 inch), ends trimmed, cut into 36 slices**
- **1 large clove garlic, peeled, cut in half**
- **¾ cup/180 g *Philadelphia* Cream Cheese Spread**
- **2 large plum tomatoes, chopped**
- **8 slices bacon, cooked, crumbled**
- **1 cup/40 g chopped lettuce**
- **¼ cup/60 ml Kraft Extra Virgin Olive Oil Aged Balsamic Vinaigrette Dressing**
- **⅓ cup/35 g Kraft 100% Parmesan Grated Cheese**

1. **Heat** barbecue to medium heat. Grill bread slices 2 min. on each side; cool.
2. **Rub** garlic onto toast; spread with cream cheese spread.
3. **Combine** tomatoes, bacon, lettuce and dressing; spoon over toast slices. Sprinkle with Parmesan.

shortcut

Use pre-baked toast rounds purchased from the grocery store.

Easy Baked Cheese & Vegetable Twist

prep: 20 min. \ total: 1 hour \ makes: 16 servings, 1/16 recipe (81 g) each

- **2 eggs**
- **125 g (½ of 250-g pkg.) *Philadelphia* Brick Cream Cheese, softened**
- **½ cup/60 g Kraft 4 Cheese Italiano Shredded Cheese**
- **3 cups/540 g frozen broccoli cuts, thawed, drained**
- **½ lb. (225 g) fresh mushrooms, cut into quarters**
- **½ cup/90 g cherry tomatoes, cut in half**
- **4 green onions, sliced**
- **2 cans (235 g each) refrigerated crescent dinner rolls**

1. **Heat** oven to 375°F/190°C/mark 5.
2. **Mix** first 3 ingredients in large bowl until well blended. Stir in next 4 ingredients.
3. **Unroll** crescent dough; separate into 16 triangles. Arrange in 11-inch/27.5 cm circle on foil-covered baking sheet, with short sides of triangles overlapping in centre and points of triangles toward outside. (There should be a 5-inch/12.5 cm diameter opening in centre of circle.) Spoon cheese mixture onto dough near centre of circle. Bring outside points of triangles up over filling, then tuck under dough in centre of ring to cover filling.
4. **Bake** 35 to 40 min. or until crust is golden brown and filling is heated through.

special extra

Sprinkle with additional ½ cup/60 g shredded cheese before baking.

Dijon Scalloped Potatoes

prep: 20 min. \ total: 1 hour 20 min. \ makes: 16 servings, ½ cup (125 ml) each

- **1 onion, chopped**
- **187 g (¾ of 250-g pkg.) *Philadelphia* Brick Cream Cheese, softened**
- **1 can (10 fl. oz./284 ml) 25%-less-sodium chicken broth**
- **1 Tbsp. Dijon mustard**
- **1½ lb. (675 g) Yukon Gold potatoes (about 4), peeled, thinly sliced**
- **60 Ritz Crackers, crushed (about 2 cups/240 g)**
- **3 Tbsp. Kraft 100% Parmesan Grated Cheese**
- **2 Tbsp. butter, melted**
- **2 tsp. chopped fresh parsley**

1. **Heat** oven to 350°F/180°C/mark 4.
2. **Cook** onions in large skillet sprayed with cooking spray on medium-high heat 5 to 7 min. or until crisp-tender, stirring frequently. Add cream cheese, broth and mustard; cook and stir 1 to 2 min. or until cream cheese is melted and sauce is well blended. Add potatoes; stir to evenly coat.
3. **Spoon** into 13×9-inch/ 33×23cm baking dish sprayed with cooking spray. Mix remaining ingredients; sprinkle over potatoes.
4. **Bake** 50 min. to 1 hour or until potatoes are tender.

special extra

For added colour and flavour, substitute 1 sweet potato for 1 of the Yukon Gold potatoes.

Creamed Corn

prep: 5 min. \ total: 10 min. \ makes: 6 servings

- **63 g (¼ of 250-g pkg.) *Philadelphia* Brick Cream Cheese, cubed**
- **2 Tbsp. milk**
- **1 can (14 fl. oz./398 ml) cream-style corn**
- **3 cups/540 g frozen corn, thawed**
- **½ cup/60 g Kraft Double Cheddar Shredded Cheese**
- **⅓ cup/60 g sliced green onions**

1. **Cook** cream cheese and milk in medium saucepan on medium heat until cream cheese is melted, stirring frequently.
2. **Add** cream-style and thawed corn; stir. Cook 4 min. or until heated through, stirring occasionally.
3. **Spoon** into serving dish; sprinkle with Cheddar cheese and green onions.

special extra

If you like a hint of spice, stir in a dash or two of hot sauce.

Easy Cauliflower & Broccoli au Gratin

prep: 10 min. \ total: 23 min. \ makes: 10 servings, ¾ cup (175 ml) each

- **1 lb. (500 g) large cauliflower florets**
- **1 lb. (500 g) large broccoli florets**
- **½ cup/125 ml water**
- **½ cup (½ of 250-g tub) *Philadelphia* Light Cream Cheese Spread**
- **¼ cup/60 ml skim milk**
- **½ cup/125 g light sour cream**
- **1½ cups/180 g shredded Cracker Barrel Cheddar Cheese Light**
- **10 Ritz 30% Less Fat Crackers, crushed**
- **3 Tbsp. Kraft 100% Parmesan Light Grated Cheese**

1. **Place** cauliflower and broccoli in 2-L microwaveable dish. Add water; cover. Microwave on HIGH 8 to 10 min. or until vegetables are tender; drain. Set aside.
2. **Microwave** cream cheese spread and milk in 2-cup/500 ml microwaveable measuring cup or medium bowl 1 min. or until cream cheese is melted and mixture is well blended when stirred. Add sour cream; mix well. Pour over vegetables; sprinkle with Cheddar cheese. Microwave 2 min. or until cheese is melted.
3. **Mix** cracker crumbs and Parmesan cheese. Sprinkle over vegetables.

note

For best results, cut the cauliflower and broccoli into similarly sized pieces before microwaving.

Desserts

Cheesecake Party Pops

prep: 15 min. \ total: 10 hours 20 min. \ makes: 42 servings, 1 pop each

- **2 eggs**
- **3 pkg. (250 g each) *Philadelphia* Brick Cream Cheese, softened**
- **¾ cup/160 g sugar**
- **1 tsp. vanilla**
- **1½ pkg. (6 squares each) Baker's Premium 70% Cacao Dark Chocolate**
- **1½ pkg. (6 squares each) Baker's White Chocolate**

1. **Heat** oven to 325°F/160°C/mark 3.
2. **Line** 13×9-inch/33×23cm pan with foil, with ends of foil extending over sides. Process first 4 ingredients in food processor until well blended. Pour into prepared pan. Bake 35 min. or until centre is set. Cool completely. Refrigerate 4 hours. Use foil handles to lift cheesecake from pan before cutting into 42 squares. Roll each square into ball; place on parchment paper-covered baking sheet. Insert 1 lollipop stick into centre of each. Freeze 4 hours.
3. **Melt** chocolates in separate bowls as directed on packages. Dip 21 lollipops in dark chocolate; return to baking sheet. Repeat with remaining lollipops and white chocolate. Drizzle remaining melted chocolate of contrasting colour over lollipops. Refrigerate 1 hour or until chocolate is firm.

Brown Sugar Cheesecake with Bourbon Sauce

prep: 20 min. \ total: 6 hours 5 min. \ makes: 12 servings, 1 piece (92 g) and 2 Tbsp. (30 ml) sauce each

- **¾ cup/180 g butter, divided**
- **1¼ cups/110 g Oreo Baking Crumbs**
- **3 pkg. (250 g each) *Philadelphia* Brick Cream Cheese, softened**
- **1¾ cups/400 g packed brown sugar, divided**
- **1 Tbsp. vanilla**
- **3 eggs**
- **½ cup/125 ml whipping cream**
- **¼ cup/60 ml bourbon**

1. **Heat** oven to 350°F/180°C/mark 4.
2. **Melt** ¼ cup/60 g butter; mix with cookie crumbs until well blended. Press onto bottom of 9-inch/23 cm springform pan.
3. **Beat** cream cheese, ¾ cup/160 g sugar and vanilla in large bowl with mixer until well blended. Add eggs, 1 at a time, beating on low speed after each just until blended. Pour over crust.
4. **Bake** 40 to 45 min. or until centre is almost set. Run knife around rim of pan to loosen cake; cool completely before removing rim. Refrigerate 4 hours.
5. **Meanwhile,** bring cream, bourbon, remaining butter and sugar to boil in saucepan; simmer on medium-low heat 7 to 10 min. or until slightly thickened, stirring constantly. Cool. Refrigerate until ready to serve.
6. **Pour** bourbon sauce into microwaveable bowl. Microwave on HIGH 30 sec. or just until warmed; stir. Spoon 2 Tbsp. over each serving of cheesecake just before serving.

Mint-Chocolate Cheesecake

prep: 20 min. \ total: 6 hours 8 min. \ makes: 16 servings, 1 piece (90 g) each

- **1 ¼ cups/110 g Honey Maid Graham Crumbs**
- **¼ cup/60 g butter, melted**
- **3 pkg. (250 g each) *Philadelphia* Brick Cream Cheese, softened**
- **¾ cup/160 g sugar**
- **3 eggs**
- **1 tsp. mint extract**
- **4 squares Baker's Semi-Sweet Chocolate**
- **½ cup/125 ml whipping cream**

1. **Heat** oven to 350°F/180°C/mark 4.
2. **Mix** graham crumbs and butter; press onto bottom of 9-inch/23 cm springform pan.
3. **Beat** cream cheese and sugar in large bowl with mixer until well blended. Add eggs, 1 at a time, beating on low speed after each just until blended. Stir in extract; pour over crust.
4. **Bake** 40 to 45 min. or until centre is almost set. Run knife around rim of pan to loosen cake; cool before removing rim. Refrigerate 4 hours.
5. **Microwave** chocolate and cream in microwaveable bowl on MEDIUM 1 to 2 min. or until chocolate is almost melted; stir. Microwave 30 sec. to 1 min. or until chocolate is completely melted and mixture is well blended, stirring every 30 sec. Pour over cheesecake; let stand 5 to 10 min. or until glaze is firm.

special extra

For stronger mint flavour, increase the mint extract to 2 tsp.

Citrus & Raspberry Cheesecake

prep: 15 min. \ total: 6 hours \ makes: 16 servings, 1 piece (85 g) each

- **1¼ cups/110 g Honey Maid Graham Crumbs**
- **¼ cup/60 g butter, melted**
- **3 pkg. (250 g each) *Philadelphia* Brick Cream Cheese, softened**
- **¾ cup/160 g granulated sugar**
- **1 Tbsp. cornstarch**
- **1 Tbsp. lemon zest**
- **3 Tbsp. lemon juice**
- **3 eggs**
- **2 cups/265 g fresh raspberries**
- **1 Tbsp. icing sugar**

1. **Heat** oven to 350°F/180°C/mark 4.
2. **Mix** graham crumbs and butter; press onto bottom of 9-inch/23 cm springform pan.
3. **Beat** cream cheese and granulated sugar in large bowl with mixer until well blended. Add cornstarch, zest and lemon juice; mix well. Add eggs, 1 at a time, beating on low speed after each just until blended. Pour over crust.
4. **Bake** 40 to 45 min. or until centre is almost set. Run knife around rim of pan to loosen cake; cool before removing rim. Refrigerate 4 hours. Top with berries and icing sugar just before serving.

special extra

Substitute 1 cup/130 g blueberries for 1 cup/130 g of the raspberries.

New York Cheesecake

prep: 15 min. \ total: 5 hours 35 min. \ makes: 16 servings

- **1¼ cups/110 g Honey Maid Graham Crumbs**
- **¼ cup/60 g butter, melted**
- **5 pkg. (250 g each) *Philadelphia* Brick Cream Cheese, softened**
- **1 cup/210 g sugar**
- **3 Tbsp. flour**
- **1 Tbsp. vanilla**
- **1 cup sour cream**
- **4 eggs**
- **1 can (19 fl. oz./540 ml) cherry pie filling**

1 **Heat** oven to 325°F/ 160°C/mark 3 if using a silver 9-inch/23 cm springform pan (or to 300°F/ 150°C/mark 2 if using a dark nonstick 9-inch/23 cm springform pan). Mix graham crumbs and butter; press firmly onto bottom of pan. Bake 10 min.

2 **Beat** cream cheese, sugar, flour and vanilla in large bowl with electric mixer on medium speed until well blended. Add sour cream; mix well. Add eggs, 1 at a time, mixing on low speed after each addition just until blended. Pour over crust.

3 **Bake** 1 hour 10 min. or until centre is almost set. Run knife or metal spatula around rim of pan to loosen cake; cool before removing rim of pan. Refrigerate 4 hours or overnight. Top with pie filling before serving. Store leftover cheesecake in refrigerator.

special extra

Omit cherry pie filling. Prepare and refrigerate cheesecake as directed. Top with 2 cups mixed berries. Brush with 2 Tbsp. strawberry jelly, melted.

Pumpkin Swirl Cheesecake

prep: 20 min. \ total: 6 hours 5 min. \ makes: 16 servings, 1 piece (89 g) each

- **18 Peek Freans Ginger Crisps (1 sleeve), crushed (about 2 cups/ 265 g)**
- **¼ cup/30 g finely chopped pecans**
- **¼ cup/60 g butter, melted**
- **3 pkg. (250 g each) *Philadelphia* Brick Cream Cheese, softened**
- **¾ cup/160 g sugar, divided**
- **1 tsp. vanilla**
- **3 eggs**
- **1 cup/260 g canned pumpkin**
- **1 tsp. ground cinnamon**
- **¼ tsp. ground nutmeg**
- **Dash ground cloves**

1. **Heat** oven to 350°F/180°C/mark 4.
2. **Mix** cookie crumbs, nuts and butter; press onto bottom of 9-inch/23 cm springform pan.
3. **Beat** cream cheese, ½ cup/105 g sugar and vanilla with mixer until blended. Add eggs, 1 at a time, beating after each just until blended. Remove 1 cup/250 ml plain batter. Stir remaining sugar, pumpkin and spices into remaining batter.
4. **Spoon** half the pumpkin batter into crust; top with spoonfuls of half the plain batter. Repeat layers; swirl with knife.
5. **Bake** 45 min. or until centre is almost set. Cool completely. Refrigerate 4 hours.

Bavarian Apple Torte

prep: 30 min. \ total: 4 hours 5 min. \ makes: 12 servings

- **½ cup/120 g butter, softened**
- **1 cup/210 g sugar, divided**
- **1 cup/130 g flour**
- **1 pkg. (250 g) *Philadelphia* Brick Cream Cheese, softened**
- **1 egg**
- **½ tsp. vanilla**
- **½ tsp. ground cinnamon**
- **4 Granny Smith or Golden Delicious apples (1 lb./500 g), peeled, sliced**
- **¼ cup/20 g sliced almonds**

1. **Heat** oven to 425°F/ 220°C/mark 7. Beat butter and ⅓ cup/70 g of the sugar in small bowl with electric mixer on medium speed until light and fluffy. Add flour; mix well. Spread onto bottom and 1 inch/2.5 cm up side of 9-inch/23 cm springform pan.
2. **Beat** cream cheese and ⅓ cup/70 g of the remaining sugar in same bowl with electric mixer on medium speed until well blended. Add egg and vanilla; mix well. Spread evenly over crust. Combine remaining ⅓ cup/70 g sugar and the cinnamon. Add to apples in large bowl; toss to coat. Spoon over cream cheese layer; sprinkle with almonds.
3. **Bake** 10 min. Reduce temperature to 375°F/ 190°C/ mark 5; continue baking 25 min. or until centre is set. Cool on wire rack. Loosen torte from rim of pan. Cover and refrigerate 3 hours before serving. Store any leftovers in refrigerator.

substitute

Substitute finely chopped pecans for the sliced almonds.

Chocolate-Vanilla Swirl Cheesecake

prep: 55 min. \ total: 5 hours 35 min. \ makes: 24 servings, 1 piece (77 g) each

- **20 Oreo Cookies, crushed (about 2 cups/265 g)**
- **3 Tbsp. butter, melted**
- **4 pkg. (250 g each) *Philadelphia* Brick Cream Cheese, softened**
- **1 cup/210 g sugar**
- **1 tsp. vanilla**
- **1 cup/250 g sour cream**
- **4 eggs**
- **6 squares Baker's Semi-Sweet Chocolate, melted, cooled**

1. **Heat** oven to 325°F / 160°C/mark 3.
2. **Mix** cookie crumbs and butter; press onto bottom of foil-lined 13×9-inch/ 33×23cm pan. Bake 10 min.
3. **Beat** cream cheese, sugar and vanilla in large bowl with mixer until well blended. Add sour cream; mix well. Add eggs, 1 at a time, mixing after each just until blended.
4. **Reserve** 1 cup/250 ml batter. Stir chocolate into remaining batter; pour over crust. Top with spoonfuls of reserved batter.
5. **Swirl** batters with knife. Bake 40 min. or until centre is almost set. Cool. Refrigerate 4 hours.

special extra

Garnish with chocolate curls just before serving. Use a vegetable peeler to shave the side of an additional square of Baker's Semi-Sweet Chocolate until desired amount of curls is obtained. Wrap remaining chocolate and store at room temperature for another use.

Gingerbread Cheesecake

prep: 30 min. \ total: 6 hours 20 min. \ makes: 16 servings, 1 piece (100 g) each

- **18 Peek Freans Ginger Crisps, crushed (about 1 ¼ cups/110 g)**
- **¼ cup/60 g butter, melted**
- **3 pkg. (250 g each) *Philadelphia* Brick Cream Cheese, softened**
- **¾ cup/160 g sugar**
- **¼ cup/60 ml molasses**
- **1 Tbsp. vanilla**
- **1 tsp. ground cinnamon**
- **1 tsp. ground nutmeg**
- **½ tsp. ground ginger**
- **¼ tsp. ground cloves**
- **3 eggs**
- **4 squares Baker's Semi-Sweet Chocolate, chopped**
- **½ cup/125 ml whipping cream**

1. **Heat** oven to 350°F/180°C/mark 4.
2. **Mix** cookie crumbs and butter; press onto bottom of 9-inch/23 cm springform pan.
3. **Beat** cream cheese and sugar in large bowl with mixer until well blended. Add molasses, vanilla and spices; mix well. Add eggs, 1 at a time, mixing on low speed after each just until blended. Pour over crust.
4. **Bake** 45 to 50 min. or until centre is almost set. Run knife around rim of pan to loosen cake; cool completely before removing rim. Refrigerate 4 hours.
5. **Microwave** chocolate and whipping cream in microwaveable bowl on HIGH 1 min; stir. Microwave 30 sec to 1 min. or until chocolate is completely melted and mixture is well blended, stirring every 30 sec. Pour over cheesecake.

Chocolate-Raspberry Thumbprints

prep: 20 min. \ total: 45 min. \ makes: 4½ doz. or 27 servings, 2 cookies (38 g) each

- **2 cups/260 g flour**
- **1 tsp. baking soda**
- **¼ tsp. salt**
- **4 squares Baker's Unsweetened Chocolate, coarsely chopped**
- **½ cup/120 g butter**
- **1 pkg. (250 g) *Philadelphia* Brick Cream Cheese, softened**
- **1¼ cups/265 g sugar, divided**
- **1 egg**
- **1 tsp. vanilla**
- **⅓ cup/115 g Kraft Pure Red Raspberry Jam**

1. **Heat** oven to 375°F/190°C/mark 5.
2. **Mix** flour, baking soda and salt. Microwave chopped chocolate and butter in large microwaveable bowl on MEDIUM 2 min.; stir until chocolate is completely melted. Whisk in cream cheese. Add 1 cup/210 g sugar, egg and vanilla; mix well. Stir in flour mixture. Refrigerate 15 min.
3. **Roll** dough into 1-inch/2.5 cm balls; coat with remaining sugar. Place, 2 inches/5 cm apart, on baking sheets. Press your thumb into centre of each ball; fill each indentation with about ¼ tsp. jam.
4. **Bake** 8 to 10 min. or until lightly browned. Cool 1 min. on baking sheet; transfer to wire racks. Cool completely.

substitute

Prepare using your favourite flavour Kraft Pure Jam.

Double-Decker OREO Cheesecake

prep: 25 min. \ total: 5 hours 40 min. \ makes: 24 servings, 1/24 recipe (84 g) each

- **1 pkg. (350 g) Oreo Cookies, divided**
- **¼ cup/60 g butter, melted**
- **4 pkg. (250 g each) *Philadelphia* Brick Cream Cheese, softened**
- **1 cup/210 g sugar**
- **1 tsp. vanilla**
- **1 cup/250 g sour cream**
- **4 eggs**
- **4 squares Baker's Semi-Sweet Chocolate, melted**

1. **Heat** oven to 325°F/ 160°C/mark 3.
2. **Process** 30 cookies in food processor until finely ground. Add butter; mix well. Press onto bottom of 13×9-inch/ 33×23 cm baking pan.
3. **Beat** cream cheese, sugar and vanilla in large bowl with mixer until well blended. Add sour cream; mix well. Add eggs, 1 at a time, beating after each just until blended; pour half over crust. Stir melted chocolate into remaining batter; pour over batter in pan. Chop remaining cookies; sprinkle over batter.
4. **Bake** 45 min. or until centre is almost set. Cool completely. Refrigerate 4 hours.

make ahead

Wrap cooled cheesecake tightly in foil. Freeze up to 2 months. Thaw in refrigerator overnight before serving.

Dark Chocolate-Hazelnut Souffle

prep: 10 min. \ total: 55 min. \ makes: 6 servings, ⅙ recipe (116 g) each

- **1 tsp. butter**
- **½ cup/105 g plus 1 Tbsp. sugar, divided**
- **6 eggs**
- **1 tub (250 g) *Philadelphia* Cream Cheese Spread**
- **1 Tbsp. hazelnut-flavored liqueur**
- **3 squares (28 g each) bittersweet chocolate, melted**
- **2 Tbsp. chopped hazelnuts, toasted**

1. **Heat** oven to 350°F/180°C/mark 4.
2. **Grease** bottom and side of 1-L souffle dish with butter; sprinkle with 1 Tbsp. sugar.
3. **Blend** eggs, cream cheese spread, remaining sugar, liqueur and chocolate in blender 30 sec. or until smooth. Blend on high speed 15 sec. Pour into prepared dish.
4. **Bake** 40 to 45 min. or until puffed and lightly browned; sprinkle with nuts. Serve immediately.

substitute:
Substitute a 1-L casserole dish for the souffle dish.

Lemon-Cream Cheese Cupcakes

prep: 15 min. \ total: 1 hour 39 min. \ makes: 24 servings, 1 cupcake (64 g) each

- **1 pkg. (2-layer size) white cake mix**
- **1 pkg. (3.4 oz.) Jell-O Lemon Instant Pudding**
- **1 cup/250 ml water**
- **4 egg whites**
- **2 Tbsp. oil**
- **1 pkg. (250 g) *Philadelphia* Brick Cream Cheese, softened**
- **¼ cup/60 g butter, softened**
- **2 Tbsp. lemon juice**
- **3¾ cups/465 g icing sugar**

1. **Heat** oven to 350°F/ 180°C/mark 4.
2. **Beat** first 5 ingredients in large bowl with mixer on low speed 1 min. or until dry ingredients are moistened. (Batter will be thick.) Beat on medium speed 2 min. Spoon into 24 paper-lined muffin cups.
3. **Bake** 21 to 24 min. or until toothpick inserted in centres comes out clean. Cool in pans 10 min.; remove to wire racks. Cool completely.
4. **Beat** cream cheese, butter and lemon juice in large bowl with mixer until well blended. Gradually add sugar, beating well after each addition. Spread onto cupcakes.

special extra

Add 1 tsp. lemon zest to frosting before spreading onto cupcakes. Garnish each cupcake with a small twist of lemon zest.

Neapolitan Cheesecake

prep: 30 min. \ total: 6 hours 20 min. \ makes: 16 servings, 1 piece (100 g) each

- **1¼ cups/110 g Honey Maid Graham Crumbs**
- **¼ cup/60 g butter, melted**
- **4 pkg. (250 g each) *Philadelphia* Brick Cream Cheese, softened**
- **1 cup/210 g sugar**
- **4 eggs**
- **2 squares Baker's Semi-Sweet Chocolate, melted**
- **1 Tbsp. vanilla**
- **1 cup/270 g frozen strawberries, thawed, drained and mashed**
- **2 squares Baker's White Chocolate**

1. **Heat** oven to 350°F/180°C/mark 4.
2. **Mix** graham crumbs and butter; press onto bottom of 9-inch/23 cm springform pan.
3. **Beat** cream cheese and sugar in large bowl with mixer until well blended. Add eggs, 1 at a time, mixing on low speed after each just until blended. Divide batter into thirds (about 2 cups/500 ml each); pour each of 2 portions into separate small bowls. Stir semi-sweet chocolate into 1 portion, vanilla into second portion and berries into remaining portion.
4. **Pour** semi-sweet chocolate batter over crust; freeze 5 min. Cover with vanilla batter; freeze 5 min. Top with strawberry batter.
5. **Bake** 50 to 55 min. or until centre is almost set. Run knife around rim of pan to loosen cake; cool completely before removing rim. Refrigerate 4 hours. Use vegetable peeler to make curls from white chocolate. Use to garnish cheesecake just before serving.

how to mash the strawberries

Use a potato masher or pastry blender to mash the strawberries.

Chocolate Elegance

prep: 20 min. \ total: 4 hours 35 min. \ makes: 14 servings, 1 piece (71 g) each

- **1½ pkg. (250 g each) *Philadelphia* Brick Cream Cheese, softened**
- **½ cup/105 g sugar**
- **2½ cups/225 g thawed Cool Whip Whipped Topping, divided**
- **6 squares Baker's Semi-Sweet Chocolate, divided**
- **1 pkg. (4-serving size) Jell-O Chocolate Instant Pudding**
- **½ cup milk**
- **¼ cup sliced almonds, toasted**

1. **Beat** cream cheese and sugar with mixer until well blended. Stir in 1½ cups/112 g Cool Whip; spread 2 cups onto bottom of 8×4-inch/21×11 cm loaf pan lined with plastic wrap. Melt 3 chocolate squares. Add to remaining cream cheese mixture along with pudding mix and milk; beat until blended. Spread over layer in pan. Refrigerate 4 hours.
2. **Microwave** remaining chocolate and Cool Whip in microwaveable bowl on HIGH 1 min.; stir until blended. Cool slightly.
3. **Invert** dessert onto platter. Remove pan and plastic wrap. Spread dessert with glaze; top with nuts. Refrigerate until glaze is firm.

Easy Dessert Dip

prep: 5 min. \ total: 1 hour 5 min. \ makes: 1¾ cups or 14 servings, 2 Tbsp. (30 ml) each

- **1 pkg. (250 g) *Philadelphia* Brick Cream Cheese, softened**
- **1 jar (198 g) Jet-Puffed Marshmallow Creme**

1. **Mix** ingredients until well blended.
2. **Refrigerate** 1 hour.

serving suggestion

Serve with assorted Christie Cookies or cut-up fresh fruit.

New York-Style Strawberry Swirl Cheesecake Squares

prep: 20 min. \ total: 6 hours \ makes: 16 servings, 1 piece (112 g) each

- **1 cup/130 g Honey Maid Graham Crumbs**
- **3 Tbsp. sugar**
- **3 Tbsp. butter, melted**
- **4 pkg. (250 g each) *Philadelphia* Brick Cream Cheese, softened**
- **1 cup/210 g sugar**
- **3 Tbsp. flour**
- **1 Tbsp. vanilla**
- **1 cup/125 g sour cream**
- **4 eggs**
- **⅓ cup/115 g Kraft Pure Strawberry Jam**

1. **Heat** oven to 325°F/160°C/mark 3.
2. **Line** 13×9-inch/33×23 cm pan with foil, with ends of foil extending over sides. Mix graham crumbs, 3 Tbsp. sugar and butter; press onto bottom of pan. Bake 10 min.
3. **Beat** cream cheese, 1 cup/210 g sugar, flour and vanilla with mixer until well blended. Add sour cream; mix well. Add eggs, 1 at a time, mixing on low speed after each just until blended. Pour over crust. Microwave jam in microwaveable bowl on HIGH 30 sec. Drop small spoonfuls of jam over batter; swirl gently with knife.
4. **Bake** 40 to 45 min. or until centre is almost set. Cool completely. Refrigerate 4 hours. Use foil handles to remove cheesecake from pan before cutting to serve.

Cinnamon Toast "Blinis"

prep: 20 min. \ total: 35 min. \ makes: 18 servings, 2 rolls each

- **1 pkg. (250 g) *Philadelphia* Brick Cream Cheese, softened**
- **½ cup/105 g sugar, divided**
- **¼ tsp. vanilla**
- **1 egg yolk**
- **1 tsp. ground cinnamon**
- **12 slices white bread, crusts removed**
- **3 Tbsp. butter, melted**

1. **Heat** oven to 400°F/200°C/mark 6. Mix cream cheese, ¼ cup/55 g of the sugar, vanilla and egg yolk with wire whisk until well blended. In separate bowl, mix remaining ¼ cup sugar and cinnamon; set aside.
2. **Flatten** each bread slice with rolling pin. Spread 1 side of each slice evenly with 1 rounded Tbsp. cream cheese mixture. Starting at short end, tightly roll up. Brush each roll with butter; roll in reserved cinnamon-sugar. Slice each roll into 3 pieces.
3. **Place** each piece, seam side down, on baking sheet. Bake 12 to 15 min. or until edges are lightly browned. Serve immediately.

jazz it up

For an extra special treat, baked rolls can be dipped halfway into melted Baker's Chocolate.

Red Velvet Cupcakes

prep: 20 min. \ total: 1 hour 14 min. (incl. cooling) \ makes: 24 servings, 1 cupcake (40 g) each

- **1 pkg. (2-layer size) chocolate cake mix**
- **2 Tbsp. red food colouring**
- **125 g (½ of 250-g pkg.) *Philadelphia* Brick Cream Cheese, softened**
- **¼ cup/60 g butter, softened**
- **3 cups/375 g icing sugar**
- **½ cup/35 g thawed Cool Whip Whipped Topping**
- **1 square (28 g) Baker's White Chocolate, shaved into curls**

1. **Prepare** cake batter and bake as directed on package for 24 cupcakes, blending food colouring into batter before spooning into prepared muffin cups. Cool. Poke hole in top of each cupcake with handle of wooden spoon.
2. **Beat** cream cheese and butter in large bowl with mixer until well blended. Gradually beat in sugar. Whisk in Cool Whip; spoon 1½ cups/375 g into small freezer-weight resealable plastic bag. Seal bag; cut small corner off bottom of bag. Insert tip into hole in top of each cupcake; pipe about 1 Tbsp. frosting into centre.
3. **Frost** cupcakes with remaining frosting; top with chocolate curls. Keep refrigerated.

Strawberry-Cheesecake Ice Cream

prep: 20 min. \ total: 12 hours 35 min. \ makes: 8 servings, ½ cup (125 ml) each

- **1 pkg. (250 g) *Philadelphia* Brick Cream Cheese, softened**
- **1 can (300 ml) sweetened condensed milk**
- **⅓ cup/85 ml whipping cream**
- **2 tsp. lemon zest**
- **1½ cups/195 g fresh strawberries**
- **3 graham wafers, coarsely chopped**

1. **Mix** first 4 ingredients with mixer until well blended. Freeze 4 hours or until almost solid.
2. **Beat** cream cheese mixture with mixer until creamy. Blend berries in blender until smooth. Add to cream cheese mixture with chopped wafers; mix well. Freeze 8 hours or until firm.
3. **Remove** ice cream from freezer 15 min. before serving; let stand at room temperature to soften slightly before scooping to serve.

Triple-Chocolate Cheesecake

prep: 20 min. \ total: 6 hours 15 min. \ makes: 16 servings, 1 piece (119 g) each

- **1¼ cups/110 g Oreo Baking Crumbs**
- **⅓ cup/40 g butter, melted**
- **1 pkg. (6 squares) Baker's White Chocolate, divided**
- **4 pkg. (250 g each) *Philadelphia* Brick Cream Cheese, softened, divided**
- **1 cup/210 g sugar, divided**
- **½ tsp. vanilla**
- **3 eggs**
- **3 squares Baker's Semi-Sweet Chocolate, divided**
- **2½ cups/225 g thawed Cool Whip Whipped Topping**

1. **Heat** oven to 325°F/160°C/mark 3.
2. **Mix** cookie crumbs and butter; press onto bottom of 9-inch/23 cm springform pan. Melt 5 white chocolate squares as directed on package; cool slightly.
3. **Beat** 3 pkg. cream cheese, ¾ cup/160 g sugar and vanilla with mixer until well blended. Add melted white chocolate; mix well. Add eggs, 1 at a time, mixing on low speed after each just until blended. Pour over crust.
4. **Bake** 50 to 55 min. or until centre is almost set. Run knife around rim of pan to loosen cake; cool completely. Meanwhile, melt 2 semi-sweet chocolate squares; cool.
5. **Beat** remaining cream cheese and sugar in large bowl until well blended. Add melted semi-sweet chocolate; mix well. Whisk in Cool Whip; spread over cheesecake. Refrigerate 4 hours. Garnish with chocolate curls from remaining white and semi-sweet chocolates.

Simply Sensational Truffles

prep: 10 min. \ total: 2 hours 10 min. \ makes: 3 doz. or 18 servings, 2 truffles (30 g) each

- **2½ pkg. (8 squares each) Baker's Semi-Sweet Chocolate (20 squares), divided**
- **1 pkg. (250 g) *Philadelphia* Brick Cream Cheese, softened**

1. **Melt** 8 chocolate squares as directed on package. Beat cream cheese in medium bowl with mixer until creamy. Blend in melted chocolate. Refrigerate 1 hour or until firm.
2. **Cover** baking sheet with waxed paper. Shape chocolate mixture into 36 balls, using about 2 tsp. for each. Place in single layer on prepared baking sheet.
3. **Melt** remaining chocolate. Use toothpicks to dip truffles in chocolate; return to tray. Decorate as desired. Refrigerate 1 hour or until chocolate is firm.

special extra

Sprinkle truffles with ½ cup chopped nuts, crushed peppermint candies and/or coloured sprinkles immediately after dipping in melted chocolate.

Creamy Lemon Nut Bars

prep: 15 min. \ total: 1 hour \ makes: 32 servings

- **½ cup/120 g butter, softened**
- **⅓ cup/40 g icing sugar**
- **2 tsp. vanilla**
- **1¾ cups/235 g flour, divided**
- **⅓ cup/30 g pecans, chopped**
- **1 pkg. (250g) *Philadelphia* Brick Cream Cheese, softened**
- **2 cups/420 g granulated sugar**
- **3 eggs**
- **½ cup/125 ml lemon juice**
- **1 Tbsp. grated lemon zest**
- **1 Tbsp. icing sugar**

1. **Heat** oven to 350°F/180°C/mark 4. Line 13×9-inch/33×23cm baking pan with foil; spray with cooking spray. Mix butter, ⅓ cup/40 g icing sugar and vanilla in large bowl. Gradually stir in 1½ cups/200 g of the flour and pecans. Press dough firmly onto bottom of prepared pan. Bake 15 min.
2. **Beat** cream cheese and granulated sugar in medium bowl with electric mixer on high speed until well blended. Add remaining ¼ cup/35 g flour and eggs; beat until blended.
3. **Stir** in lemon juice and zest. Pour over baked crust in pan. Bake 30 min. or until set. Remove from oven; cool completely. Sprinkle with 1 Tbsp. icing sugar; cut into 32 bars.

substitute

Prepare as directed, using lime juice and grated lime zest.

Banana Split "Cake"

prep: 15 min. \ total: 5 hours 15 min. \ makes: 24 servings, 1 piece (93 g) each

- **1½ cups/110 g Honey Maid Graham Crumbs**
- **⅓ cup/40 g non-hydrogenated margarine, melted**
- **2 pkg. (250 g each) *Philadelphia* Brick Cream Cheese, softened**
- **1 cup/210 g sugar**
- **1 can (14 fl. oz./398 ml) crushed pineapple in juice, drained**
- **6 bananas, divided**
- **2 pkg. (4-serving size each) Jell-O Vanilla Instant Pudding**
- **2 cups/500 ml cold milk**
- **2 cups/150 g thawed Cool Whip Whipped Topping, divided**
- **1 cup/100 g chopped pecans**

1. **Mix** graham crumbs and margarine; press onto bottom of 13×9-inch/33×23cm pan. Freeze 10 min.
2. **Beat** cream cheese and sugar with mixer until well blended. Spread carefully over crust; top with pineapple. Slice 4 bananas; arrange over pineapple.
3. **Beat** pudding mixes and milk in medium bowl with whisk 2 min. Stir in 1 cup/75 g Cool Whip; spread over banana layer in pan. Top with remaining Cool Whip. Refrigerate 5 hours.
4. **Slice** remaining bananas just before serving; arrange over dessert. Sprinkle with nuts.

substitute

Prepare as directed, topping with Baker's Semi-Sweet Chocolate curls rather than chopped pecans.

Tiramisu Bowl

prep: 20 min. \ total: 2 hours 20 min. \ makes: 16 servings

- **1 pkg. (250 g) *Philadelphia* Brick Cream Cheese, softened**
- **3 cups/750 ml cold milk**
- **2 pkg. (4-serving size each) Jell-O Vanilla Instant Pudding**
- **2½ cups/225 g thawed Cool Whip Whipped Topping, divided**
- **48 Nilla Vanilla Wafers**
- **½ cup/125 ml brewed strong Maxwell House Coffee, cooled, divided**
- **2 squares Baker's Semi-Sweet Chocolate, grated**
- **1 cup/130 g fresh raspberries**

1. **Beat** cream cheese with mixer until creamy. Beat in milk and pudding mixes. Stir in 2 cups/150 g Cool Whip.
2. **Line** 2½-L bowl with 24 wafers; drizzle with ¼ cup/60 ml coffee. Top with half each of pudding mixture and half of the chocolate. Repeat all layers.
3. **Top** with remaining Cool Whip and raspberries. Refrigerate 2 hours.

how to easily grate chocolate

Unwrap chocolate squares, leaving each square on paper wrapper. Microwave on HIGH 10 sec., then begin grating.

Creamy Lemon Squares

prep: 25 min. \ total: 3 hours 53 min. \ makes: 16 servings, 1 square (53 g) each

- **1 cup/130 g Honey Maid Graham Crumbs**
- **½ cup/115 g flour**
- **¼ cup/55 g packed brown sugar**
- **¼ cup/60 g cold non-hydrogenated margarine**
- **1 pkg. (250 g) *Philadelphia* Light Brick Cream Cheese Spread, softened**
- **1 cup/210 g granulated sugar**
- **2 eggs**
- **2 Tbsp. flour**
- **3 Tbsp. lemon zest, divided**
- **¼ cup/60 ml fresh lemon juice**
- **¼ tsp. Magic Baking Powder**
- **2 tsp. icing sugar**

1. **Heat** oven to 350°F / 180°C/mark 4.
2. **Line** 8-inch/20 cm square pan with foil, with ends of foil extending over sides. Mix graham crumbs, ½ cup/ 115 g flour and brown sugar in medium bowl. Cut in margarine with pastry blender or 2 knives until mixture resembles coarse crumbs; press onto bottom of prepared pan. Bake 15 min.
3. **Meanwhile,** beat cream cheese spread and granulated sugar with mixer until well blended. Add eggs and 2 Tbsp. flour; mix well. Blend in 1 Tbsp. lemon zest, juice and baking powder; pour over crust.
4. **Bake** 25 to 28 min. or until centre is set. Cool completely. Refrigerate 2 hours. Sprinkle with icing sugar and remaining zest just before cutting into squares to serve.

PHILADELPHIA Handy Tips

HOW TO SOFTEN CREAM CHEESE

- Place completely unwrapped package of cream cheese in microwaveable bowl.
- Microwave on HIGH 15 sec. or just until softened.
- Add 15 sec. for each additional package of cream cheese. Depending on the wattage of your microwave you may need to add more or less time.

HOW TO MEASURE CREAM CHEESE

- Each 250 g package of PHILLY Brick or tub yields about 1 cup of cream cheese.

HOW TO STORE CREAM CHEESE AND CREAM CHEESE FROSTED CAKES

- Always store in refrigerator. For bricks that have been opened, rewrap tightly in plastic wrap.
- Cakes filled and/or frosted with cream cheese icing should be stored in the refrigerator.
- Freezing is not recommended.

HOW TO MELT CREAM CHEESE

PHILLY melts! Scoop a few spoonfuls of PHILLY tub or small cubes of PHILLY brick and follow these helpful hints to melt your PHILLY into sauces, soups, casseroles, and more.

- Add a few spoonfuls of PHILLY spread (or cubes of softened PHILLY brick) to warm sauce or soup and stir or whisk until cream cheese is completely melted.
- Add ½ cup/125 g of PHILLY spread (or cubes of softened PHILLY brick) to a skillet containing ½ to 1 cup/125 ml to 250 ml of hot milk or broth. Stir or whisk constantly until cream cheese is melted. Add ½ cup/125 g of PHILLY spread (or cubes of softened PHILLY brick) to 3 cups/750 g of hot cooked mashed potatoes and stir until combined.

HOW TO SUBSTITUTE ONE PHILLY FOR ANOTHER

- PHILADELPHIA Cream Cheese Flavoured varieties add the same creamy flavourful richness to dishes as regular PHILADELPHIA Cream Cheese. Try varieties like PHILADELPHIA Herb & Garlic or Dill Cream Cheese for a simple flavour twist.
- For all of the same great flavour and creaminess, but 44% less fat than regular PHILADELPHIA Cream Cheese, PHILADELPHIA Light Cream Cheese can easily be substituted into your favourite dishes.
- In recipes, generally 125 g of cubed cream cheese is about equal to ½ cup of cream cheese spread.
- It is not recommended to substitute PHILADELPHIA Cream Cheese Spreads (tub) in baked items like cheesecakes or breads.

PHILADELPHIA Handy Tips

CONSEILS

POUR RAMOLLIR LE FROMAGE À LA CRÈME :

- Déposez un paquet de fromage à la crème PHILADELPHIA déballé dans un bol allant au four à micro-ondes.
- Chauffez le fromage au four à micro-ondes à température élevée pendant 15 secondes ou jusqu'à ce qu'il soit ramolli.
- Ajoutez 5 secondes de plus pour chaque paquet de fromage à la crème supplémentaire. Selon la puissance de votre four à micro-ondes, vous pourriez devoir prolonger ou réduire le temps indiqué.

POUR MESURER LE FROMAGE À LA CRÈME :

- Chaque paquet de fromage à la crème PHILADELPHIA en briques ou en pot donne environ une tasse de fromage à la crème.

POUR CONSERVER LE FROMAGE À LA CRÈME ET LES GÂTEAUX AVEC GLAÇAGE AU FROMAGE À LA CRÈME

- Conservez toujours le fromage à la crème au réfrigérateur. Si le paquet a été ouvert, enveloppez-le soigneusement de pellicule de plastique.
- Les gâteaux garnis de glaçage au fromage à la crème doivent être conservés au réfrigérateur.
- La congélation n'est pas recommandée.

POUR FAIRE FONDRE LE FROMAGE À LA CRÈME :

Le fromage à la crème PHILADELPHIA peut fondre! Utilisez quelques cuillérées de fromage à la crème PHILADELPHIA en pot ou quelques petits cubes de fromage à la crème PHILADELPHIA en brique et suivez ces quelques conseils pour faire fondre votre PHILADELPHIA dans vos sauces, vos soupes, vos plats mijotés et bien d'autres mets.

- Ajoutez quelques cuillérées de fromage à la crème PHILADELPHIA tartinable (ou de cubes de fromage à la crème PHILADELPHIA en brique ramolli) à des sauces ou des soupes chaudes, et mélangez ou fouettez jusqu'à ce que le fromage soit complètement fondu.
- Ajoutez ½ tasse de fromage à la crème PHILADELPHIA tartinable (ou de cubes de fromage à la crème PHILADELPHIA en brique ramolli) à un poêlon contenant ½ ou une tasse de lait ou de bouillon chaud. Mélangez ou fouettez constamment jusqu'à ce que le fromage à la crème soit fondu. Ajoutez ½ tasse de fromage à la crème PHILADELPHIA tartinable (ou de cubes de fromage à la crème PHILADELPHIA en brique ramolli) à 3 tasses de purée de pommes de terre chaude et mélangez jusqu'à ce que le fromage à la crème soit complètement incorporé.

POUR SUBSTITUER UN TYPE DE FROMAGE À LA CRÈME À UN AUTRE

- Le fromage à la crème PHILADELPHIA aromatisé donne à vos mets le même goût riche et crémeux que le fromage à la crème PHILADELPHIA ordinaire. Essayez nos variétés comme le fromage à la crème PHLADELPHIA Fines herbes et ail ou le fromage à la crème à l'Aneth pour donner un goût novateur à vos mets.
- Pour obtenir le même goût délicieux et la même texture crémeuse, mais avec 44 % moins de gras, remplacez le fromage PHILADELPHIA ordinaire par du fromage à la crème PHILADELPHIA léger dans tous vos mets préférés.
- Dans les recettes, en général 125 g de fromage à la crème en cubes représentent environ une ½ tasse de fromage à la crème tartinable.
- Il n'est pas recommandé de substituer le fromage à la crème PHILADELPHIA tartinable (en pot) dans les recettes de pâtisserie (gâteau au fromage ou pain).

index

BEEF & PORK

Chocolate Elegance **222**

Chocolate-Raspberry Thumbprints **212**

Chocolate-Vanilla Swirl Cheesecake **208**

METRIC CONVERSION CHART

VOLUME MEASUREMENTS (dry)

1/8 teaspoon = 0.5 mL
1/4 teaspoon = 1 mL
1/2 teaspoon = 2 mL
3/4 teaspoon = 4 mL
1 teaspoon = 5 mL
1 tablespoon = 15 mL
2 tablespoons = 30 mL
1/4 cup = 60 mL
1/3 cup = 75 mL
1/2 cup = 125 mL
2/3 cup = 150 mL
3/4 cup = 175 mL
1 cup = 250 mL
2 cups = 1 pint = 500 mL
3 cups = 750 mL
4 cups = 1 quart = 1 L

VOLUME MEASUREMENTS (fluid)

1 fluid ounce (2 tablespoons) = 30 mL
4 fluid ounces (1/2 cup) = 125 mL
8 fluid ounces (1 cup) = 250 mL
12 fluid ounces (1 1/2 cups) = 375 mL
16 fluid ounces (2 cups) = 500 mL

WEIGHTS (mass)

1/2 ounce = 15 g
1 ounce = 30 g
3 ounces = 90 g
4 ounces = 120 g
8 ounces = 225 g
10 ounces = 285 g
12 ounces = 360 g
16 ounces = 1 pound = 450 g

DIMENSIONS

1/16 inch = 2 mm
1/8 inch = 3 mm
1/4 inch = 6 mm
1/2 inch = 1.5 cm
3/4 inch = 2 cm
1 inch = 2.5 cm

OVEN TEMPERATURES

250°F = 120°C
275°F = 140°C
300°F = 150°C
325°F = 160°C
350°F = 180°C
375°F = 190°C
400°F = 200°C
425°F = 220°C
450°F = 230°C

BAKING PAN SIZES

Utensil	Size in Inches/Quarts	Metric Volume	Size in Centimeters
Baking or Cake Pan (square or rectangular)	8×8×2	2 L	20×20×5
	9×9×2	2.5 L	23×23×5
	12×8×2	3 L	30×20×5
	13×9×2	3.5 L	33×23×5
Loaf Pan	8×4×3	1.5 L	20×10×7
	9×5×3	2 L	23×13×7
Round Layer Cake Pan	8×1½	1.2 L	20×4
	9×1½	1.5 L	23×4
Pie Plate	8×1¼	750 mL	20×3
	9×1¼	1 L	23×3
Baking Dish or Casserole	1 quart	1 L	—
	1½ quarts	1.5 L	—
	2 quarts	2 L	—